C0-ASO-988

Humor
And
A Little Bit More

By
Taylor Reese

AAcorn Books
Micaville, NC

Copyright © 1999 by Taylor Reese

All rights reserved. No part of this book may be reproduced or transmitted in any form or by any means, electronic or mechanical, including photocopying, recording, or by any information storage and retrieval system, without permission in writing from the author or publisher.

Cover concept by Linda Murray
Cover Design by Morris Publishing
Book Design by Linda Murray

Published by:
AAcorn Books
P.O. Box 647
Micaville, NC 28755

ISBN: 0-9663666-3-8
Library of Congress Card Number: 99-73216

Printed in the United States of America by:

Morris Publishing
3212 East Highway 30 – Kearney, NE 68847
800-650-7888

Other books by Taylor Reese

**HUMOR Is Where You Find It
(Look No Further)**

And

Written with Co-author Jack R. Pyle:

RAISING WITH THE MOON – The Complete Guide To Gardening – and Living – by the Signs of the Moon.

YOU AND THE MAN IN THE MOON – The Complete Guide to Using the Almanac

This book is
dedicated
to all readers
but
especially those who like
Humor
and
"a little bit more."

ACKNOWLEDGMENTS

Becky Poteat Sims
Charles Edwin Price
Edith Keys
Susie & Steve Painter
Eileen McCullough
Jack Kerr
Ruth Gibson

Art Work From Microsoft Publisher 98

CONTENTS

Long-Distance Hauling

While signing books at a B. Dalton bookstore, a lady approached and wanted to purchase a book for her husband. In the course of the conversation I inquired as to her kind of work. She said that she worked in the headquarters of a long-distance truck-hauling firm where her husband was employed. And then she added that for years she and her husband were team drivers in long-distance hauling from coast to coast. They had made the trip over and over, week in and week out.

"It was a long haul," she said, "but we loved it. And we always traveled with our little poodle. His name was Randy Travis."

As our conversation continued, she became more generous with her interesting experiences, and I asked if during her cross-country travels with him if she and her husband each had their own CB handle.

"Oh, yes," she said.

"And what was your handle?"

"Little Miss Muffet."

"And his?"

"You won't believe it," she said, "but his is 'Potty Chair.' He said he calls himself that because on the road he has to listen to so much crap from the other drivers."

Just Remember

On the evening before her wedding the next day, the bride-to-be was very nervous as they were going through dress rehearsal.

"Look, Gloria," said the minister, "Tomorrow is going to be the most beautiful day in your life. Don't worry about it. Just try to relax and be yourself. As you start down the aisle, it will help if you just take it one step at a time and concentrate.

"Here's what you do: When you are walking down, focus your eyes on the aisle, concentrate, and if you still feel nervous, raise your head slightly and look straight at the altar. And, finally, be sure to try to concentrate on the very first hymn you hear. If you do that, I think you'll lose your nervousness."

"I'll try," she said.

On her wedding day the church was filled with family and friends, and as she was walking down, many near the aisle heard her mumbling, "Aisle, altar, hymn; aisle, altar, hymn; aisle, altar hymn."

The Ultimates

Two fellows were talking and one said to the other, "You know something, I'm a very fortunate man. My wife is just great in so many ways; she really treats me like a king."

"Oh, yeah?" said his buddy.

"Yes. Every morning she serves me breakfast in bed."

"I think that's good," his buddy said. "But my wife treats me like a God. Every morning she comes up with a burnt offering."

The Newspaper Man

My newspaper delivery man is extremely reliable and prompt in delivering the paper, and always puts it in a wrapper when the weather is inclement. He also has a great sense of humor.

In the interest of recycling and conservation, I save the wrappers and when I have a stack I put them in the paper box for pickup.

On one occasion I left a bundle and put a note stating that he might want to use them again.

The morning after he picked them up, I found a note along with the day's paper: "My wife thanks you and says that it is good to recycle, and that should extend to husbands."

The Toothpick

A fellow worker and I were leaving the local restaurant. He had a toothpick in his mouth, and just as we stepped outside the door onto the sidewalk, three ladies--all beautifully attired and definitely of the uppercrust variety-- were walking by. One lady stared at my friend with more than just a disapproving look; it was a look of "How tasteless and rude can you be, picking your teeth on the public street like that."

My friend, sensing her disapproval, said, "Lady when you pay my dental bills you can tell me how to take care of my teeth."

The Sedative

After spending quite a hectic weekend with his wife's relatives, and enduring all the noise and confusion, he and the wife were finally in the car enroute to their own home.

He looked over at her and said, "Honey, I love you, and I love your family, but it is the only gathering that I go to where I have to take Valium before I arrive, while I am there, and when I leave."

4

Bumper Stickers - No. 1

While traveling south on Interstate 95, headed for Florida, I fell in behind a luxurious motor home, towing a medium-sized car. On its back bumper were the words:

I go to where I'm towed to

And here are others noted while traveling

Normal people worry me

I tried to contain myself but escaped

We need more like you--off the road

No Strings

It was a cold winter night as the wife and husband sat across from one another before the fireplace. "Wouldn't you think," she asked, "that we could live as peacefully as Fido and Meow? Just look at them. They never fight."

And the husband said, "No, they don't, but try tying them together and then see what happens."

As We Go Through

At 10 we're eager to learn

At 15 we know it all

At 20 we're even smarter

At 25 we're divorcing

At 30 we're on the second divorce

At 35 it's her children, his children and "our" children

At 40 it's another divorce

At 45 it's a new interest

At 50 it's golf

At 55, the 45 interest has become the woman of all times

At 60 social life is great

At 65 Medicare becomes an entitlement

At 70 it's more Medicare and now medicine

At 75 it's at least one operation

At 80 it's medication, many medications

At 85 it's closer to the One above

At 90 to 100 it's time to begin again.

Maybe Later

While empanelling a jury for a highly publicized case, both counsel for the plaintiff and the defendant were trying to elicit information that would enable them to seat jurors that they thought would be unbiased.

"Sir," asked the plaintiff's attorney, "you realize this case is a very emotional one for both the wife and the husband, seated over here at these two tables?"

"Yes, sir, I do."

"And we may need to ask you some questions that you might consider personal but, as a prospective juror, we hope that you will come forth with truthful answers. I know that you will."

"Yes, sir."

"Mr. Brown, do you own a home?"

"Yes, sir, I do."

"Are you married or single?"

"I am married, sir. I have been for three years."

"And, Mr. Brown, have you formed or expressed an opinion in this matter?"

"No, sir, I have not, not in three years. That's really not long enough."

***

Someone said, "I started out with nothing and still have most of it."

***

There's one good thing you can say about the egotist: He doesn't talk about other people.

One humorous gent from western Virginia loves to quote short lines of poetry, and offers this one, but comments before quoting that none of us are perfect, "Not even me," he says.

> I got a gal in Cumberland Gap;
>
> She's got a boy that calls me Pap.

And he also offered another, "at no charge," he   says:

> My daddy was a Cannon,
>
> And I'm a son-of-a gun.

Plus:

> Around the curve the car was whizz'n,
>
> The funeral was hers, the fault was his'n.

And on the more serious side:

> With every rising of the sun
>
> Think of the day as just begun.

Which Way

Back in 1976 one clever writer said that we had to choose between Republican Capitalism and Carter's brand of Popularism.

And then he added, "You know, people still don't understand the difference, because with Republican Capitalism man exploits man, and with Popularism it's the other way around."

Stay Out Of The Sunshine

"Keep that hat on," my mother said. "How many times have I got to tell you that if you don't wear the straw hat you'll blister your face.

"And besides that, the sun makes your hair grow faster, and I'm the one that has to cut it." (Although there was a barber shop in the small town, my mother had a good set of clippers and scissors and combs, and she cut my father's hair and all of her children's.)

Those words were indelibly enmeshed in my brain for as early as I can remember. Mama was right.

I remembered, though, when I was about 8 or 9, that if what she had said was right--that the exposure to the sun would make your hair grow faster on the head--why wouldn't the same thing apply to other parts of the body. And I had noticed that my older brothers already had hair on other parts of their body, but I didn't.

I approached my next older brother--about five years' difference--and asked why he had hair in that area and I didn't.

"Because," he quickly offered, "you're not old enough. It will grow just like mine as you get older."

"But mama said that if I kept my hat off my head it not only would blister my face but make the hair on my head grow faster."

"Trust me," my brother said, "you'll get hair in the area soon enough. You don't need to know any more than that."

Now, that wasn't sufficient for my curiosity or patience, so I decided to take the matter, in my own hands.

Often during that summer I would slip off to an open space in the wooded area way behind our house. I would go there fully clothed, straw hat included, and I would keep my shirt on but pull my pants down so that the pubic area was exposed. I made sure that my straw hat covered all my face, so as not to burn it.

Throughout the summer, I made clandestine trips to the woods, offering up only to God and the sun, that exposed area of my body. I checked each time I got a bath to see if there was any sign of even the slightest "sprouting" of fuzz "down there." Nothing.

So, summer came and went. My diligent effort to become like my older brothers had borne no obvious change. It was after that episode that I realized my brother was right. So, I decided to let time and nature proceed at their own pace, and I'm still letting nature take its course as the hair on my head begins to go.

Fertile Ground

While autographing at a book store, a customer, a mother I presumed, followed by five small children--stairstep in size--approached and was looking at my book. We began to talk and she evidenced interest in vegetables and other health foods.

I asked, "Do you, by any chance, grow your own herbs?"

"No," she quickly replied, "Can't you tell? I grow children, and this is only half of them."

Compliments Do Help

"Well, thank you for the compliment," the lady said, after a short conversation about health and appearance. I had remarked that I thought nature had done an excellent job of putting all her parts together.

"Well, I agree with you, but that was sometime ago, and now a lot of the parts need replacing."

The Times Are Changing

A black writer friend of mine loves to tell humorous stories on herself. She is a great citizen in her town in Florida, always actively participating in the worthwhile projects, projects that further the goals and aims of the area.

She told me of an incident which she says occurred many years ago, in the days when there were labeled water fountains in most public establishments. They, like the rest rooms, were marked, one for the blacks and one for the whites.

She said she was shopping on the second floor in one of the town's better department stores, and then stepped on the escalator and rode down to the first floor. Nearby were the two water fountains: One labeled "Black," the other "White."

She wanted to see what would happen if she drank from the "White" one, so she walked over, took a few drinks. As she straightened up and looked around, a middle-aged white woman was staring at her and said, "You know you're not supposed to drink from that fountain; the Black one is over there," pointing toward the one with the Black sign on it.

"Oh, really?"

"Yes," said the lady, emphatically.

And my friend said, "Well, don't you *know* I can't read?"

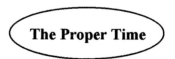

The Proper Time

It was late, and I knew it was time to stop proofreading the manuscript when I picked up the dictionary on my desk to check the spelling of the word "popularism."

I was halfway down the P's when it occurred to me that it would not be found in that particular volume, A through O.

Not Bad Advice

Some of us will remember the occasion when President Lyndon Johnson was participating in an economic summit conference. The Japanese official had told him that the United States should devalue the American dollar, and Johnson is reported to have said, "Up your yen."

An Accounting

The husband of quite a few years had each week dutifully turned over a substantial portion of his paycheck to his wife. She was to pay the bills, and a great portion of the monies she was given was earmarked for groceries.

Finally, the husband, a bit dubious about how the generous amount of money earmarked for groceries was being spent, mustered the courage to ask, "Sweetheart, do you mind telling me where all that money goes that's earmarked for groceries?"

"Not at all," said the wife. "Just go into the bathroom, strip down, and look in the mirror."

Resistance

"You know," said the elderly gentleman, "I'll be 100 tomorrow, if the Lord spares me until then. And, to my knowledge, I don't have an enemy in the world."

"Remarkable," said the stranger sitting beside him on the park bench. "I'm sure He will spare you until then, but do you have a recipe for such accomplishments: a long life and not an enemy in the world?"

"I sure do. I've outlived every doggoned one of them."

Statistics Don't Lie

And then another old gent, when asked on his 100th birthday to what he attributed his long life, said, "Well, I guess the main reason is that I was born in 1899."

Check It

Sign on the outside of the weight therapist's office door:

Advice for the thin: Do not eat fast.

Advice for the fat: Do not eat, fast.

Mother-In-Law Category

Necessary Information

The undertaker in a distant city telegraphed a man with the message that his mother-in-law had died and asked if he should bury, embalm or cremate her.

The man said, "All three. Let's take no chances."

Too Late?

The woman called and notified police of her husband's disappearance.

"I'm sorry to hear that ma'am. Is there any message we should give him if we should find him?"

"Yes. Tell him that mother didn't come after all."

Gratuitous Suggestion

The wife looked over at her husband and said, "Honey, last year we sent mother a chair for Christmas. What do you think we ought to do for her this year?"

The husband snorted loudly, "Electrify it."

Generous Contribution

The solicitor knocked on the door and said, "Could you please donate something to the Old Ladies' Home?"

"Indeed I will," said the man. "Help yourself to my mother-in-law."

A Misfire

"Mr. Jones, you say it was an accident that you shot your wife?" asked the judge.

"Yes, your Honor, it was. She got in front of my mother-in-law just as I pulled the trigger."

The Truth Will Out

The farmer's mule kicked his mother-in-law to death, and a large crowd attended the funeral. During his comments, the preacher said that she must have been very popular.

"They're not here for the funeral," one of the men yelled out, "they're here to buy that mule."

* * *

Economics

When asked why she shot her husband, the
poor wife said,
"Well, Judge, I couldn't afford a divorce."

Honesty

"How do you like my voice?" inquired the singer.

With some hesitancy the accompanist said, "Well,
Madam, I've played the white keys and I've played the black
keys. But this is the first time I've seen anyone who could
sing in the cracks."

It All Depends

Many things are said and done at
family reunions, and my family's was
and continues to be no exception.

I remember an occurrence at one
of them more than sixty years ago
during which nearly a hundred of us
were gathered at Grandma and Grandpa's place, way out in
the country. Their house was situated on a considerable
amount of acreage and set back quite a distance from the
unpaved road. Their lane, like the road to their house, was
unpaved.

With that groundwork laid, I refer to the humorous story
told in my first humor book about my grandfather who took a
walk out his lane and found a condom, and the conversation
that occurred between him and one of his sons.

When the book came out I sent copies to several relatives. One of them called and said that she didn't remember that happening at all.

"Well," I said, "it surely did. You know when you have a hundred or so people milling around, talking--some in groups of various sizes--you can't hear or be aware of everything that is being said or done."

"I'm aware of that," she said, "but I never missed a reunion back in those days and I just don't remember it."

"So, we have a different recollection," I said. "Let's just let it go at that."

And we did. The matter was not discussed again; however, a month or so later I was in her home where a number of people had gathered for the evening. The subject of my first humor book came up, and I happened to have been sitting next to one of her sons.

He leaned over and whispered, "Mama tore out Page 95 in your book, the one about Grandpa's Discovery."

"You have to be kidding," I said.

And then I turned to his mother and said, "Surely, you didn't?"

"Didn't what?" she asked.

"Tear out Page 95 in my humor book."

"I certainly did," she replied. "I don't remember it happening, and besides, it's not funny."

"Well," I said, "that's the best advertisement I can get." And we let it drop at that.

Now, if she acquires a copy of this second book of humor, I don't know how she will react, but since I have mentioned no names, only she and a few others will know who it is that failed to see humor in the situation, or even accept the fact that the incident did occur. In any event, it was a funny little story in the first book...*and still is.*

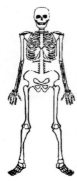

Illusion

Just as a drunk was stumbling by, a fat lady stepped up on a pair of scales that were not working properly. They showed her weight at only 75 pounds when it was quite obvious she weighed much, much more than that.

The drunk looked over and said, "My God, woman, you must be hollow."

Bumper Stickers - No. 2

**Mothers don't know it all
But the rest is unimportant**

**If at first you don't succeed
Try again--on the left**

**I can't go to work today
Voices are telling me
To go home and clean my guns**

**Don't steal
The government hates competition**

No Chance

With the political climate the way it is today, it reminds me of the occasion when the news station was interviewing a local politician, and was asked if he felt he had influenced public opinion.

The seasoned fellow immediately came up with, "Well, no, I don't, not really. As I see it, public opinion is like the old mule I once owned. In order to keep up the appearance of being in charge, I had to watch the way he was going and then follow closely."

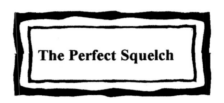

The Perfect Squelch

I like the funny I heard about the Democratic Convention being held in a large city, and there had been a fantastic banquet one evening at one of the hotels.

The next day a rather prominent Republican met one of the Democratic delegates in the lobby and said, "I understand there were some Republicans at the dinner last night."

"Oh, yes," replied the Democrat, "one waited on me."

Try It

Ole John was griping to his neighbor about the world in general being so far gone.

"Well, if you really feel that way, John, why don't you just pretend each morning when you get up that that will be your last day."

"Really?"

"Yes, and then one day you'll be right."

Informative

One witty neighbor never fails to take advantage of an audience, be it in the backyard, the house, on the street or in the car. He constantly throws short takes or leads you into a corner.

"Say," he asked the neighbor lady on the other side of me, "did you realize that marriage is a three-ring circus?"

"And I suppose you are the ringmaster?"

"No, I'm not, but it is a three-ring circus: engagement ring, wedding ring, and the last, suffering."

Mother-Of-Pearl

"Counsel, have you anything further to offer?"

"Yes, Judge, I do," replied Mr. Lozier.

"And so do I, Your Honor," said Mr. Swift.

"All right," said the Judge. "Before we continue I would like to make a few comments to Roger and Josephine Lacken.

"I'm sure counsel for each of you has explained that this is the final hearing in the divorce suit you filed, Mr. Lacken, against your wife, Josephine. I want to compliment both of you for the manner in which you, and your counsel, have conducted yourselves throughout the several hearings we have had. They involved some mighty complicated and tedious issues. While on some occasions the situation became quite difficult because of the animosity between you two, overall, you are to be commended.

"Mr. Lozier, you may proceed."

"Your Honor, eighteen years ago, shortly after my client,

Roger Lacken, married Josephine, he gave her a precious gift, especially precious to him. He gave Josephine a small metal box covered with beautiful mother-of-pearl.

"This box had been given to him by his mother. His father had given it to her shortly after they were married. Now, Your Honor, even before that his grandmother had received it as a gift from his grandfather--Mr. Lacken's grandfather--on the day they were married."

"Do you have the box?"

"No, sir, Judge, my client does not. Mrs. Lacken has it. That is the problem. This box has been so closely tied in with Mr. Lacken's family for so long that we respectfully ask the Court to order the defendant, Josephine Lacken, to return it to Mr. Lacken."

"Mr. Swift?"

"Thank you, Your Honor.

"Mrs. Lacken, if you will, tell the Court what you told me earlier today."

"Judge, Roger gave me that box, as his lawyer said, shortly after we were married, and he told me it was to keep my special things in, jewelry and stuff. And, Judge, I have done that. I kept his love letters, photos, and things like that. It meant, and still means, a lot to me, Your Honor, and I think I should be allowed to keep it."

"Counsel, do you or Mrs. Lacken have the box here today?"

"Yes, Judge, it is here in this bag. This is it."

"All right. Mr. Lozier, do have anything further?"

"No, sir."

The Judge looked at the plaintiff. "Mr. Lacken, I'm aware of the sentimental attachment you have for this beautiful box, but after having given it to her, your wife, under such circumstances, why do you feel that you are entitled to its return?"

"Well, as my lawyer mentioned, Judge, it has been in my family for so long. And when I gave it to her, I loved her. I still love her. I thought our marriage would last. I certainly did not think, after all these years, that she would take up with another man. And, Your Honor, she kept that from me. I found that out quite by accident, that she was 'running around.'

"We have raised two nice boys: John, 16, and Paul, 14. They are staying with her right now. I love those boys and they love me. But now that we are divorcing because of this, she obviously has no place for me in her life. And I think that box, which has been in my family for three generations, should continue to be in my family. That's why I want it back, to keep it in my family."

"I understand your feelings, Mr. Lacken, but by your own admission, it was given to your wife openly and freely. It has been in her possession for eighteen years, or thereabout; and as you heard her say, she has kept some of her personal belongings, her special things, in it. I think it means a lot to her. It is something she has used, she says, throughout the years, and I think it should continue to be hers.

"So, I am going to rule that Mrs. Lacken may keep the mother-of-pearl box given to her by her husband, Mr. Lacken, shortly after their marriage.

"Does either counsel have anything further to offer?"

"No, sir, Judge," said Mr. Lozier.

"We do not, Your Honor," answered Mr. Smith.

"Mr. Lozier, have you prepared the order of dissolution?"

"Yes, Your Honor, I have. Here it is."

"I will sign it," said the Judge.

As the judge was signing the order, he said, "Now, I think both of you have had excellent representation, and I wish you happiness in the future."

Mr. Swift and his client left the Judge's chambers. Mr. Lozier and Mr. Lacken sat out in the hall and talked for a few minutes.

As Mr. Lacken was descending the courthouse steps, he saw Josephine standing alone midway down.

"Roger," she called, "will you come over here a minute?"

"Yes," Roger replied.

They met near the center. Josephine reached in her bag, and pulled the mother-of-pearl box from it.

"Roger, you deserve this. Take it. And here is the key. Even though we are finished with one another, you heard the Judge say I could keep it. But it is from your family, and I know how you feel. It's yours," and then she handed it to him.

"Oh, thank you, Josephine. You know I will always love you."

She ignored his comment, and said, "Please don't open it until you get home."

"I won't."

When he arrived he placed the box on the dining room table, pulled up a chair and took the key from his pocket.

- - -

The following morning Josephine sat at the table in her apartment, reading the newspaper.

She called out, "Paul, are you in there?"

"Yes, mother."

"Wake up John, and you two come in here."

They walked in and sat across from her.

"John, Paul, your father's dead."

Both bowed their heads.

"Listen," the mother said, "here's what it says in the paper: 'Lacken was apparently killed by an explosion. Metal fragments and shattered pieces of mother-of-pearl were found scattered throughout the dining room of his home. Police are investigating; however, at this point foul play is not suspected."

The Building

The farmer was engaged in putting up a building as the casual observer came by.

"What are you building?" asked the gentleman.

"Well," said the farmer, "if I can rent it, it's a rustic cottage nestled 'neath a few tall pines. If I can't, it's a cowshed."

Just For Safety's Sake

The mother said to her daughter, in quite an admonishing tone, "Didn't I tell you not to let that man come over to your apartment last night? You know how things like that worry me."

And the daughter said, "But, mother, I didn't. I went over to his apartment; now let his mother do the worrying."

Superstition

At the prison, a ministerial visitor asked one of the inmates, "Young fellow, how did you happen to come to this sad place?"

"Well, sir," replied the convicted man, "you see in me today the unhappy victim of the unlucky number 13."

"Indeed," said the visitor, "and how is that?"

"Twelve jurymen and one judge, sir."

Suspicion

The husband answered the phone, listened for a moment and then said to the caller, "How in the world would I know? I mean, why don't you just call the coast guard or weather station?" And then he hung up.

"Who was that?" asked the wife.

"I don't know," he said. "Some man wanted to know if the coast was clear."

In Travel

As is the usual case when one travels across country by car, stops are made for rest and relief. On one of the rest room walls some kind person had written:

"My travel agent is Jesus Christ."

And just below, in a different handwriting, someone had scribbled:

"To warmer climes, I presume."

Still a bit farther down, another had penned:

"Be sure He hasn't booked you for the southern tour."

Encouragement

While driving through a small town in the east, I noticed a sign outside a weight-loss establishment which read: "Lose 10 pounds by Christmas." As I looked to my right and directly across the street from the weight-loss place there was a bakery. The enticing sign read: "House of Pies"

Help

One type of person I have a great deal of admiration for is the elder gentleman who is retired but takes a part-time job to supplement his income.

I was in the local grocery store one morning and ran into such a retiree.

As he was bagging my groceries, I noticed his name tag and it read: "John."

I said, "John, how are you today?" and he replied, "Why, I'm fine; how about yourself?"

"Likewise," I said, and then added, "Guess how I knew your name?"

"That's not difficult," he responded. "You see, I'm quite famous. There are quite a number of places around the country that carry my name. There is the St. John's River in Florida, the St. John's Cathedral, and many more. There are many churches throughout the country that carry my name, too, and all named after me."

And then he said, "There was a fellow in here the other day, and he asked me, "Well, John, what are you doing working in here?"

I said, ""I'm one of God's deciples down here to take care of you.""

Be Kind

I was griping about the rabbits eating my garden, and the neighbor, always a kind and thoughtful soul, said, "Well, just remember this: They may not be as intelligent as humans, but they are as determined in their ways--about as much, I expect--as the other inhabitants on this earth."

Solitaire

As I sat in the car ready to leave I waved goodbye and said, "Solitaire, I'll be back to see you soon."

She nodded, flashed her dark eyes, and I knew what she was thinking: "Hurry back; we have lots in common." And we did. She was a llama that thought she was a human being.

Born three months earlier on a cold and windy night, Solitaire's mother took one look, smelled her, and turned away. She refused to be suckled, and obviously wanted nothing to do with her newborn. Could it have been that she sensed a difference in her child? Who knows? But Solitaire was destined to win the heart of every person she met.

Her owner immediately became the "mother," and began to use her expert knowledge in handling the unfortunate situation. Under normal conditions, the baby gets colostrum milk from the mama llama. Nature planned it that way so that the mother's first milk contains exactly the proper balance of nutrients and antibodies needed to help the little one grow and develop. This aids in building an essential immune system. Without this natural progression, such protection sometimes takes months.

Solitaire caught cold twice and was given shots of

penicillin. The congestion was so severe she could not take her bottle, but as soon as Vicks VapoRub was put in her nostrils she responded within minutes.

She was bottle-fed every four hours around the clock, and for weeks her diet consisted of only Meyenberg canned goat milk. (It is easy to digest.)

Although she was placed in her own "cottage," she preferred to come into the garage and, had she been permitted, would have come into the house. And still would.

Solitaire has never met a stranger. She walks right up to them, smells and looks, and then waits to be petted. When she is happy, she makes a kind of soft humming noise; when impatient, louder hums; and on the rare occasions when annoyed, yet another, a grunting/growling. To the experienced ear, each noise is distinctly different.

Her biological mother and a dozen other llamas are kept in a different area. For weeks every time she was given the opportunity to be with her own, each of the others were accepting, but not mama; she would have nothing to do with her child.

As the weeks went by, Solitaire followed her adopted mother wherever she went around the homestead. On the daily visits to see the relatives, she would stop and look them over. Although mama stood and stared during this time, it was nearly three months before she approached her offspring. And often, as Solitaire was fed her bottle before them, they, being by nature curious, would stand and watch her drink her meal. On one occasion much later it was particularly heartening to see her mother stare at her child. When Solitaire finished drinking the milk, together the two turned and walked away, each nudging the other as they ambled side by side. Finally, they were beginning to bond.

As weeks went by and it was feeding time for her relatives,

she would meet her mother and the others on their side of the bridge. She would sometimes hesitate and then turn to Moses, a younger llama cousin, and they would rub noses. Moses obviously loved it. (He had acquired that name because on the day he was born he got too close to a nearby pond, slid in, and had to be pulled from the bulrushes.) She would then join her adopted mother, occasionally stopping and looking back at her relatives. They seemed to say "Goodbye, Solitaire, at least for awhile."

They wanted her to become one of them, and Solitaire wanted to, but she was torn. The acceptance and obvious appreciation for the human nurturing conflicted with the innate feeling of llama kinship which was beginning to kick in.

She is a big girl now, five months, but continues to be partially fed from the bottle, two daily, 32 ounces each, morning and evening. Canned Carnation evaporated milk has replaced the goat milk. And although she doesn't know it, she is now a little too big to lie on the throw rug just inside the garage. She uses it off and on during the day while resting, despite the fact that her rear is off the rug most of the time.

Solitaire continues to take walks with her adopted mother. When the two are returning to her cottage, she will often stop, look back at her biological mother and the others, as if to say, "Come with us; it's a better life over on this side of the bridge." But her relatives never do, and there is a reason for that:

Although it is built over a swift-flowing creek that poses no threat, the bridge that Solitaire crosses to reach her family has an inch of open space between each of the planks, and they, like most other cloven-hoofed animals, do not cross such a structure. There is a fear. They follow her to the bridge, stop short of stepping onto the first plank, and stand, just looking. Solitaire, however, has no fear because since shortly after birth she began to follow alongside her adopted mother as she walked across the bridge, never for a moment realizing that she was not like the others in that respect.

It is obvious that the relatives look forward to her visits, no doubt aware that when the day is over she will again return to her own quarters and a different life style.

She now nibbles on fresh blades of grass, green buds here and there, and some oats that are regularly fed to her relatives and peers. She will still need the twice-daily milk for several more months.

Solitaire is unique in that she--for the present at least--remains a human llama, or llama human. Statistics reveal, however, that as a result of being bottle fed, she will one day openly manifest the usual llama traits, and in some rare instances will become less gentle. But for the time being she has shown all the humans with whom she has come in contact that she is one of them; and those humans with whom she has come in contact are perfectly willing to leave it just that way.

+++++ Diagnosis ++++++

An elderly retired nurse friend of mine came from a few miles away to visit and brought some chicken soup, the kind that doctors say is good for a cold.

When she came in I was coughing and complaining and said, "Jo, I don't know what in the world this is, but it has held on for more than two weeks now, and I can't shake it. It really makes me feel lousy."

"I'm sorry to hear you've been ill; I didn't know about it until just yesterday. Have you had this before?" she asked.

"Yes, I have. Several years ago I had something just like this, and it, too, hung on and on for a long time."

"Well, then," she said, "you've got it again."

The Wind Does Blow

A delightful elderly couple, long-time friends, came by to visit. After a few hours they rose to leave, and as they stepped outside the door, a brisk wind was blowing. The husband, always a joker, and with very little hair left, said, "This wind is awful; it's blowing my hair."

Quick as a flash his wife said, "Which one is it, Sweetie, No. 16 or No. 17?"

What Will Happen

After hearing some unpleasant words exchanged between his mother and father, the six-year old asked, "Mama, if you die and go to heaven, do you think daddy will be there?"

"Not if I can help it," she said.

Tax - There Is A Way

Many years ago a lawyer friend of mine told me of an old gentleman that lived down in Florida, in the backwoods of the Okeechobee area. He said the old fellow was fed up with the government interfering with his life. In fact, he had never filed an income tax return.

When the IRS found out about it they began sending him letters. He ignored them, one after another. Finally, the IRS decided to approach him in person, and when the area agent knocked on the door the old fellow opened it and said, "Yes?"

The agent said, "Sir, I'm (name deleted). I'm from the Internal Revenue Service, and here is my badge and other credentials. I'd like to talk with you for a moment."

"Go right ahead," the old man said.

"We understand you have not paid your taxes for many years, and you have declined to fill out the required tax form."

"That's right, and I ain't going to, either."

"Well, sir, you realize, of course, that you can get yourself into a lot of trouble by not doing that, don't you?"

"Oh, yes, that's what they tell me. But you see, I ain't never filled out them forms; I don't know how to fill out them forms, and I ain't never gonna fill them out, 'cause I cain't."

And then he offered more fodder for the agent:

"Now if you want me to pay any taxes, you can just go right over there to that big old trunk you see sitting in the corner, that one right over there, and you just lift up the lid. In there you will find all my bills, everyone of my canceled checks and the receipts. Now, if you want, you can take the trunk and all, and when you have sorted it out, figured it out, you just let me know how much I owe you, and I will pay it. But I ain't going to do your work for you 'cause I cain't."

Although this allegedly occurred many years ago, I am sure many of us today feel just about like the old fellow and would be tempted to follow his feelings about the matter. Where are the reforms we hear about?

Word Definitions

The teacher asked her students to think of words that might be challenging to other classmates. And when they finished that exercise, the teacher said, "All right, I'll ask one now.

"Charles, my word is 'recuperate.' Think of that word now. I guess your father goes to work every day?"

"Yes, ma'am, he does."

"And when he finishes working, is he tired?"

"Yes, ma'am, he is."
"And then when night comes what does he do?"
"That's what my mother wants to know."

Oxymoron

Given the opportunity

To accept that which is to be

Man will every time

Seek the other

And thus live

In constant contradiction.

"I Do"

While signing books at a storytelling festival, two gentlemen were standing speaking to one another while their wives were farther away listening to a storyteller. Neither of the gentlemen appeared interested in what was going on.

One of the men said to the other, as he looked toward the two wives, "I'll tell you, let's face it, they'll drag you to anything."

And the other replied, "Yes, I agree. Oh, well, that's the penalty we have to pay when we say, 'I do' They hadn't taken *obey* out of the ceremony when I married."

Non-Invasive Surgery

After running a number of tests and examining her physically, the doctor said, "Mrs. Jones, I hate to tell you this, but you need a by-pass."

"Oh, no," she cried, "surely not that."

"Yes," said the doctor. "You need to bypass desserts, bypass all fried foods and bypass too much sitting."

Grade Level

"You see," said the neighbor to her friend, "that boy next door always brings home a wet report card."

"Wet?"

"Yes, wet; and he even does it on days that may be fair, absolutely no rain, nor storm or anything."

"I don't understand," said the friend.

"It's always below 'C' level."

The Salesman

The slick country salesman had a reputation for selling to everybody, and especially to farmers. He stopped at one home way out in the country, where he saw an old farmer standing near the fence looking at his large herd of cattle.

"Hello, sir. My name is Roland Roberts, and I am with the Sales Equipment Company down yonder aways. I saw you standing there admiring your cattle."

"Well, yeah, I was. Ain't they a pretty head of cattle?"

"They sure are, and I have just the gadget here that will help you keep a record of your herd.

"Sir, they call this the farmer's best friend when it comes to keeping a record of the crop sales, the costs, and the number of animals, cows and all that, on your farm. It is called a calculator, and it will relieve you of all the headache that goes into keeping a record in your head, or taking the time to write down all the figures. You know, you've got a lot of cattle here, and you may not even know the number of cattle you do have."

"Now, what did you say you called it?" asked the unschooled gent.

"Sir, it's called a 'calculator.'"

"Uh-huh," grunted the farmer. "Well, I'll tell you this: I know exactly how many hogs, how many sheep and how many cows I have, and I sure don't need no cow-culator to count any of them. And most of all, a cow-culator to count my head of cattle."

Window Shopping

My aunt and uncle were walking down the street arm in arm late one afternoon, and, as often was the case, my aunt turned lose my uncle's arm, to look into one of the store windows. As he stood to the edge of the sidewalk, she stood looking at the merchandise on display in the window.

When she had fulfilled her thirst for the stop, she backed away from the window just at a time when another gentleman came walking along. As he was abreast of her, while still facing the store window, she just reached out and stuck her arm under his.

My uncle saw the incident, winked at the man. So my aunt and the stranger were walking down the street, she not realizing it wasn't her husband's arm. Finally, my uncle saw her jerk the gentleman's arm--as she had done many times with her husband--and realized that she had wanted a response to something she had said. Hearing none, of course, she was prompted to jerk the arm again.

When there was no response, she looked up and saw the arm she had been holding did not belong to her husband.

"I'm sorry," she said to the gentleman, and my uncle was just about to die laughing, as he watched, following a few feet behind the two of them.

"Ma'am," the cooperative gent said, "that's all right. I wasn't going to object if your husband didn't."

 Not Quite Sure

"What caused your divorce?" asked the nosy neighbor as he got to know the new neighbor a little better.

"Well, if you want the truth, I'll tell you. I thought I was in love but I was in heat."

"In other words," said the neighbor, you were in lust. I know; I've been there."

"Young man," said the elder gent to the young fellow who thought he had it all, "I used to do that until I aged out."

"Oh, I see," said the young fellow. "You mean I will eventually get to that point where I will age out?"

"Oh, yes, certainly, if you live long enough."

The Raincoat

It was a rainy day and I had brought no raincoat. While signing books under the portico of the building where people were coming and going, as I sat at a table protected from the inclemency, one lady exited the building, looked over at me, but did not appear as if she were going to check out my books.

"Would you like to sell that beautiful raincoast?" I asked.

"How much will you offer me?"

"Oh, twice what you paid for it." I said, jokingly.

She hesitated, and quickly I said, "It was a gift from your husband, wasn't it?"

She shook her finger at me, laughed, and continued her trek outside.

Don't Curse

One spiffy looking lady walked up to the signing table, took a look at my book and then asked me, "What did the fish say when he hit a concrete wall?"

"I don't know," I said. "What did the fish say when he hit the concrete wall?"

"Dam." And then she promptly turned and left the table.

Knowledge

The uncle of two young boys had listened to them for almost a week, while they were visiting his wife and him. They had really put him through the mill, with never-ending prattle. Both nephews were bright and had never-ending questions, and, in many instances commented on the uncle's sage advice.

Finally, the uncle had had just about enough. He said, "You know something, you guys are spoiled. You want too much money. Do you know what I was getting when I married your aunt?"

One of the nephews jumped in with, "No, and I'll bet you didn't either."

Indecision

After the morning services, one gentleman stayed behind as the others departed. When the minister approached him to see if he could be of help, the fellow said, "Preacher, it's not you; it's the whole setup. I am just not sure how I feel about religion in general. Sometimes I think it's a bit more than I can swallow."

"Well," said the minister, "I'm sorry to hear that. You will concede, though, that some day you are going to die?"

"Oh, yes, sir, that I am willing to concede. We all are."

"That's right. And when you do, there is a choice, you know: You are going to either go up or go down. Now, which would you prefer?"

There was a moment's hesitancy, and then the gentleman said, "Preacher, let me think about it, and I'll be back next Sunday."

Why?

"I was shocked to hear that you broke off the engagement. It's usually the woman who does that, Robert. What happened?"

It's quite simple, Jake; she wanted to get married."

How

"Tell me, father, how do they catch lunatics?"
"Now, that's an easy one, son. They use lots of face powder, fancy dresses, and many smiles."

Age

The old gent was sitting on the park bench when a young fellow came and sat beside him. They began talking about life in general, and the old guy said, "Well, I'll tell you, I went to see my doctor just last week, and I told him that I must be getting old.

"The doctor asked me, 'Why do you say that?'

"I said, 'Because it takes me longer to sit than it does to get tired.'"

"Chippie" the Chipmunk

Though blind at birth with skin silk-soft
And helpless, too, for quite awhile,
His mother sees he eats now oft
Until he grows up right, in style.

He wears a coat of basic brown,
With stripes that run on head and side,
Which makes him look he's dressed for town
Like one who's out to seek a bride.

So once he's grown and on his own,
He takes his place among the rest
As he begins to search the zone
To find that one, the one who's best.

They burrow deep into the earth
To make a home of many rooms.
It always has a storage berth
To hide the nuts plus more legumes.

And, yes, there's space for nights of sleep,
As well as corners for the dump.
Though winter finds him down quite deep
For him it does not cause a slump.

He hibernates when it is cold,
But wakes to eat and then re-naps.
And when the Spring at last unfolds
There comes from two to eight more chaps.

Appearance Means A Lot

As the local undertaker in a small town sat waiting for his car to be repaired in the service station, he was chatting with several other local men, all having a good time exchanging tales.

One of the old-timers looked over at the undertaker and said, "You know something, you're the only person I know in town who shakes more hands than a politician."

And then he added, "Tell me something: How can you stand there at the entrance to the funeral home dressed in a $500 suit, a $250 pair of shoes and a $100 necktie and try to put on a sympathetic face?"

Trifling

Is he the trifling piece

You really want to keep?

Or should you now release

The lazy bum we call "The Creep"?

Resistance

When men begin to age and mellow

You expect them to sometimes bellow,

But it takes an exceptional fellow

To resist starches, sweets and Jell-O.

41

Togetherness

Darling, though we've spent

Our lives together,

And people say we are inseparable,

I can't help being jealous.

I lack essential trust.

I know that most of the time

We work in harmony.

Usually, you go first

And I'm content with being last.

At times you even go alone,

Though return very soon.

To most, we look alike,

And in many respects

Are treated the same.

But still, despite all this,

I hate the thought that most

Prefer you instead of me.

It's always, "Pass the salt,"

But seldom, "And pepper, too."

Misplanted

I saw my wife as part of life,

Unfortunately, not my own.

You see, 'twas strewn with fuss and strife

Because of seeds we'd previously sown.

Hearsay

My mother said I was not dumb,

But then stopped short of saying bright.

She sorta left me hanging numb:

The brain, she said, had suffered blight.

Our Elephants

Now we have the elephants from Asia,
And they are the species Elephas Maximus.
I wonder if they suffer from dysplasia,
Or if they're really one of us.

Then we have the genus from Africa,
The species Loxodonta Africana.
They stay away from the "traffica,"
And seldom eat the peeled banana.

Advice

The young fellow was up before the judge for having hit his wife. They had been in an argument and she called him words he thought were insulting to his mother. He slapped her and she fell down.

The judge found him guilty of the offense, sentenced him, and then said, "Son, don't ever hit a woman unless you hit her with the back of your hand, and then you can swear you didn't know she was there."

Syrah

I sat in comfort without dress,
And gave little thought to duress.
But at the door I heard a knock
By some cute lassie in tight frock.

And then I dressed so quickly
You could tell I was not sickly.
But as I opened the solid door
She greeted me with a bit more.

It was a bottle of Syrah
Chantovent-Prestige from afar.
I took it in my hand and said,
"Come in; I'll not ask you abed."

To which she quickly replied,
"It's the hotel that has supplied
"You with this little memento,
"Not I, you ugly old hippo."

Frankness

    The young grandson visiting his grandparents said, "Grandma, Grandpa makes a sound like a frog."

    "Yeah, he does," she said, "and when he finally croaks I'm moving to Florida."

An Effort

An elderly gentleman offered his wife some sage advice, or so he thought:

We have our differences

And we have our samenesses,

But through our sanity

And advanced age

Will come a cohesion

Which bonds.

"I'm not sure you're right," said the wife, "for it seems at times one of us lacks at least one of the above."

What Is The Technique?

Writers not only write their books but more often than not, they do a great deal of promoting with the help of the publisher. As a result, the innovative tactics used by some of the writers themselves might surprise you.

One told me about an experience he had had while waiting at his dentist's office. He said he had taken his own book with him--a book of humor, I might add--and sat quietly as he began reading some of his works.

He said he would read a piece to himself, begin smiling at its content and eventually laugh out loud. On one occasion the woman sitting next to him look over and said, "It must be funny."

"It is," he said. "Read that one right there," and he handed her the book. She read it and began laughing.

"You're right; it is funny. Who wrote that book?" And then she looked at the front cover and said, "Ray Splendor. I never heard of him."

The writer, to keep her from identifying him with the book, since his picture was on the back cover, quickly suggested that he would help her find the publisher's name in case she wanted a copy. And so he took the book and read her the address and full information, including the price, and also told her it was probably available at local bookstores.

A minute or two later the doctor's nurse opened the door to the reception room and called out, "Ray Splendor."

He looked over at the lady who had read the piece, smiled, and went on to get his dental work done.

He said that a few weeks later he received word from the publisher that six copies had been order by a woman, along with a letter telling about her experience at the doctor's office.

Not So Bright

The fellow, heavily in debt, did not know how he was going to come out of it. Then the thought occurred that he could have the house insured, burn it down, and that would take care of the matter.

He called a local agent, spoke with him about getting

insurance for the house, and as not to appear too anxious, reluctantly decided he would take out the insurance.

The anxious salesman said, "You might also be interested in our flood insurance. For the next 45 days we have a special sale on that."

"No, no, I don't think I'd be interested," said the owner. "I don't know how to start a flood."

The Quick Transition

Upscale friends of mine have their regular home in Washington, D.C., where the husband is an executive in a large firm. He always wears the expensive suits, shirts and ties, and is just the epitome of the middle-aged, top management executive.

He and his wife also have a cottage on a lake in nearby Virginia. When weekend circumstances permit, the two escape from the hustle and bustle of the big city of Washington and drive to their lakeside cottage.

On one occasion they arrived late on Friday afternoon. The husband immediately changed clothes, and came out of the bedroom wearing his sloppy old fishing clothes.

The wife watched as he stepped out of the house and started down the steps toward the lake.

"Sweetheart," she said, "that's an awful looking outfit. You've got much better everyday clothes that you could wear and look a lot more presentable."

"This will do," he said.

"I'll tell you, darling," she said, "you can revert to nothing quicker than anybody I've ever known."

Service Duty

I, like hundreds of thousands of others, was called to do my part for my country during World War II. And, once inducted, a part of that was the basic training. It included the marching, drilling, and for many the menial duties of pulling guard duty, K.P. and other assignments.

But, having had experience in civilian life as an administrative/clerical person, I decided the best way to escape the guard and K.P. duty was to offer my services in the headquarters wherever I might be stationed. Typists were in short supply, and especially those with office experience.

However, the Service tried to be fair and share their duties equally. This, I quickly realized, would mean that I would be pulling KP and Guard duty. And so I devised a little scheme whereby whenever I would transfer to a new location, I would square away my personal belongings, and then as soon as time would allow, go to the Headquarters and ask if I could use one of the typewriters to write a letter home to the family.

In every instance I was immediately granted permission.

I would take my sheets of paper, go in and sit at the typewriter and write routine material that you learn in basic typing class, such as, "Now is the time for all good men to come to the aid of their country" or "The quick brown fox jumped over the lazy dog's back."

This I could do at rapid speed. And often, out of my peripheral view I could see the staff personnel looking over, and obviously listening to the rapid rat-a-tat-tat. They were impressed with the speed with which I was writing--allegedly, at least--the letter to my family.

And without fail, the following morning when we had to line up for duty, the Sergeant would call out the various last names, such as: Smith, report for Guard Duty at such and such a location; Jones, report for KP duty, and on and on. And then the Sergeant would say, "Reese, report to Headquarters."

Of course, I acted as if I couldn't possibly imagine why I was being "summoned" to Headquarters.

And when I reported in, the officer would usually say something to this effect: "Private Reese, the sergeant told me this morning that you were in here yesterday writing a letter to your family on that typewriter over there."

"That's right, sir," I would answer.

"Well, as you probably know, we are short of typists, and we could certainly use your services. How about it?"

"I would be delighted to help, sir."

And so it went over and over. As a result, I never once pulled Guard or KP duty during my three years of service.

In Court

When asked if he had ever before appeared as a witness in court, the man said, "Yes, Your Honor, I have."

"Do you remember in what suit?"

"Yes, sir; it was my brown double-breasted one."

The Right Word

When asked by a friend to what he attributed his extraordinary success as a door-to-door salesman, the guy said, "Well, I attribute it to the first five words I say when a woman opens the door: 'Miss, is your mother in?'"

Only When Necessary

A high school group was taken abroad on a student program, to learn more about the Alps. One afternoon the teacher accompanying the group said to the man showing them around, "Oh, my, that's a dangerous precipice over there. Wouldn't you think they would erect some type of warning--a sign or something?"

And the guide said, "Yes, it is dangerous, and they did keep a warning sign up there for nearly five years and no one fell over, so they took it down."

Might As Well

The old farmer was out in the back yard setting up several beehives, and his neighbor yelled across, "Whatcha fixing to do, raise some bees?"

"Yep, why not?" replied the guy. "I can't see going through life and missing anything, and so far I've been stung in every other way."

Three Caskets

Three bronze caskets rest on biers at the foot of the altar. The conservative exteriors are calming, and the white interiors cushion three of the small town's best-known citizens. Except for the space taken up by the pews, family sprays and floral arrangements crowd the church, evidence of the mourners' feelings.

Although no one attending shows alarm, some of those filing by note different expressions on the faces of the deceased as they rest in silent repose: On one, a grimace; another, a faint smile; and the third, contentment. All victims of a tragic accident.

Miss Agnes Angela is dressed in white silk. A high collar conceals her pendulous neck skin. Bissy Moore, much younger, and in pink, wears matching gloves and pearl earrings. The third, Devoyd Deyton, is dressed in a dark blue suit, white shirt and striped blue tie.

The newspaper notice lists 3 p.m. as the time for the joint service for these townspeople. As I step inside the church filled with funereal fragrance, I glance at my watch. It is exactly 3. This is their day, their final hour on earth. And in a coupe of hours it will all be said and done.

I take a seat in the back row, so as not to disturb those already seated before the appointed time. I sit quietly and listen to the pastor offer kind words on behalf of each of them, with appropriate inflections and gestures.

Miss Angela had been the church treasurer. Her many years of service are appreciated, at least they were until the building fund was suddenly depleted. Some said she kept too much for herself. But the pastor doesn't speak of that. People are human.

Bissy Moore has been the organist. Her musical talent

was unique; she was loved by all the townspeople, young and old. She had been a pillar in the community, despite the rumor that she was a member of a questionable group not sanctioned by the church hierarchy and the town's more staid leaders.

Devoyd Deyton, although small in stature, had been the epitome of a town leader, involved in worthwhile projects for the young, the old, the poor, the well-to-do. If a cause needed assistance, he was always there.

All three, side by side, have kind and generous words spoken about them. I look at my watch and note that time is passing as the music begins, knowing this is their last hour. "Nearer My God to Thee" is always a favorite for people in small towns. And "How Great Thou Art" leaves everyone convinced--at least for the hour--that Heaven is the only place.

Kind words never hurt. Miss Angela was a good person, he said, even though she may have momentarily weakened. No one is perfect. He emphasized her good deeds, played down her weaknesses. God does forgive, he said.

Bissy Moore has praise heaped upon her, despite the rumor of her questionable connections. Her replacement will be difficult. Not every musician, especially one of her young age, can play with such reverent feeling and spiritual magnificence. God will certainly use her for His choir. Besides, this glorious addition will benefit others who later enter Heaven.

Devoyd Deyton has done much good throughout his life. The pastor said so, and nobody disagrees. God will use him to counsel others, to be His helper. All three will wear crowns once they are inside the Gate. The music begins again, "Just a Closer Walk with Thee." And then the final prayer, a combined prayer for all three: two good people who might have erred, one who did not, but all human, and only God can truly forgive us for our sins. And He does.

The mourners stand as the biers are rolled down the aisle and the caskets placed in the hearses. Most of the congregation follow to the cemetery and watch as each casket is put on its placer.

Though brief, more loving words from the pastor, and the Mayor offers fitting cliches of regret. Then, as the caskets are lowered, each in nearby plots, a final plea from the pastor: "God, have mercy on their souls, for we now place them in Your gentle care."

As I turn to leave, I look at my watch. It is exactly 4:59. Now all is said and done. The families and friends walk to their cars and return home.

Three townspeople, all good: one in shame shortly before her demise, one tainted by association, and one outstanding, are now gone. Good Christians. The pastor said so.

The town will continue. It always has. Life is that way. But compassion and loyalty are integral parts, and today that was demonstrated.

Tomorrow the new treasurer will handle the funds; the new organist will play just as well, and may belong to a more acceptable group. Or, she may not. And the person who succeeds the gentleman will be just as kind and generous. The town will go on being the town: **human**. It has a destiny, and it will live out that destiny.

Proper English

"My last name is Vowell, Sarah Vowell," said the young girl as she handed her application to the young manager when applying for a job at the "fast food" chain.

"Vowell, did you say?"

"Yes."

"Oh, now I see it here."

"Yes, just like the vowels of the alphabet, only with two Ls, not one."

"Okay. Then your mother must be an English teacher?"

"No, but she is constantly harping at me."

Compensation

The middle-aged couple approached the table where I was autographing the first humor book. She was a broad-hipped woman, and not overly endowed in the breast area. He, on the other hand, had thinning hair. As she held a copy of the book in her hand, reading to herself and smiling, at one point began to laugh.

I said, "What is that? Where are you reading from?"

She said, "Page 81, the one titled "Lacking," and then she handed it to him and said, "Here, read that one at the bottom there."

(For clarity, it is here quoted:

No one knows the trouble I've seen,
Nor do they really care.

It's not that I'm fat or lean,
It's less and less of hair.

He read it to himself, grinning along the way, and then said, "We'll take it. I know there must be one in there that fits her."

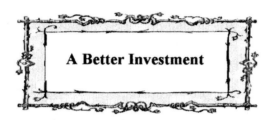

A Better Investment

While autographing at a chain book store in a large mall, there was at the same time a popular car show going on, right out in the middle of the long mall. In the center of the walkway, just 15 feet from me, was one of the latest model Mercedes.

People were milling around, and many would come up and read the price tag and then move on to another car. However, quite a few did stop and look it over, and then you would see them speak between themselves--obviously man and wife. Occasionally the sales person would show up and explain some of the features

On one occasion I noticed a couple that kept looking over in my direction. When I finally made eye contact I held up my humor book. They stepped over, and I said, "Just take a look. It's far less expensive that what you are looking at over there. You are bound to benefit from it, and it certainly doesn't cost you anything to operate, plus, it will last a lot longer." They laughed.

The wife said, "You're right, and it will make my husband

a lot happier. Not that the book is so good--I don't know about that--but it is a good deal.

"Let me have three. I want one for myself and one for my oldest sister. She has a great sense of humor. And the other one I will give as a gift to someone."

Now, whether or not they eventually purchased the Mercedes, I don't know, but they did not reappear on the screen as long as I was there.

Some Excuses

If, per chance, you are a writer and have occasion to autograph your books in various book stores, you might consider not signing near the end of the month, and particularly if your work is slanted toward those of Social Security age. Too many of them use an excuse not to buy that goes something like this:

"No, not today. My check won't come in until the 3rd. I can get it here later, can't I?"

"Oh, yes. They carry my book all the time, and it will be a signed copy. Although, I can't put an inscription in unless I'm here."

"Oh, that's all right. I will get it after the 3rd."

And then you have the looker who winds up asking you, "How long will you be here?"

"Only one more hour, ma'am."

"Good. I'll be back," she says, as she turns to walk away.

But you know from experience that neither of them will be back for your book.

Bumper Stickers - No. 3

As I pulled up to the post office I noticed an old beat-up junker pulling in beside me. When I got out of my car and walked passed, I noticed the bumper sticker:

No, this is not an abandoned car

Does this one sound familiar? It was on the back of an old car.

I can't believe it's not better

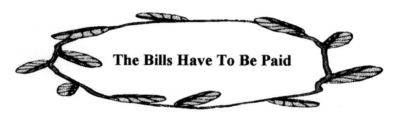

The Bills Have To Be Paid

Grandpa was an honest man, a kind man, liked by all his friends and neighbors. And in the early days, families often "ran a bill" at the local store. Periodically, he would go in and settle up. Never a problem. Although the following caused no change in the way he and the merchant did business, it did afford an anxious moment, when Grandpa had his say.

He walked in, told the store owner that he wanted to settle up. The owner pulled the account file and told him the amount.

"I didn't realize it was that much," he said.

"Well, here is each individual item listed and the date and amount of each purchase."

"Let's see," said Grandpa. He took the sheet, looked it over and asked, "What are these three items here?"

The store owner said, "Those are items Dowell, your son, came in and bought. Here, let me show you. Right there. One is cigarettes, and there is some candy. And here is some hair oil and shaving lotion. And there's another one for candy, cigarettes and soda crackers and pork and beans."

Grandpa, who had been patient, said, "Well, you realize, of course, I never gave you authorization to allow him to put anything on my bill. Only my wife and I can do that."

The owner said, "Well, sir, he is your son, and I had no qualms at all about letting him have the items there. If I had known there would be an objection on your part, I certainly would not have extended the credit and put it on your bill."

Without any hesitation Grandpa said, "He made those charges, not me, so you collect from him, not me.

"How much is the bill without those?"

The owner deducted those and gave him the amount, and Grandpa paid his rightful share.

Now, we will never know just how Grandpa handled it with his son Dowell, but something tells me he might well have squared the matter posthaste, and maybe in a manner not using money.

The Sentencing

The only vice the man did show
Was that of vagrancy.
He had few clothes and one peso,
No thought of truancy.

He told the Judge he had no bail
That would allow him free,
And that he'd gladly try travail
Until the trial to see

That he was not a liar too
Despite objection from
The counsel there all dress in blue
With looks that were quite glum.

"Sui generis," said the Judge
"To each and all around.
"This is de minimis, Old Fred,
"I will not you impound.

"Instead, you will, and very soon,
"Enjoy Fantasia
"While on this great long honeymoon
"We call Euthanasia."

Definitions: "sui generis" - of its own kind
      "de minimis" - small thing

Identification

After staring at me while waiting to catch a plane at the airport, a young teenage boy asked, "Are you Robert Aiken Smith?"

"No, I'm not; I'm Taylor Reese."

And then with a shrug of his shoulders, he said, "Oh, well, everybody has to look like somebody," and walked on.

The Rat Ride

A delightful friend of mine was telling of an experience she had as a child. She had two pet white rats which she adored. A train trip was coming up and the rats were definitely not to go. But my friend had a brilliant idea:

"I'll put them in a shoe box, punch small holes in the box here and there, so that they can get air, and then I will close the lid and nobody will know the difference."

Reluctantly, her mother agreed to the "undercover" arrangement, but cautioned her about the necessity for being careful and ever-watchful.

They boarded the train for a six-hour ride to visit a relative. She placed the box down beside her seat, and would occasionally slip a piece of cookie to them. On one occasion, she held open the top a little too far and out jumped Rice and Roni. She said they were named that because from the time they were little both would eat cooked rice, and they loved macaroni.

My friend, a tiny child of some four years, was terrified, but she collected herself and began to search around. Everyone in the train car became aware of the problem, and although several ladies put their feet up on the seats, many thought it funny and joined in the search.

Now, neither Rice nor Roni could be found. The conductor, of course, made his usual trek through each car, and even he was enlisted to help. Although, he seemed a bit annoyed, he did think it was funny.

It was more than an hour before Rice and Roni were found, and not in the car they had been riding in with their keepers. They were found in the next car. Apparently, when the various people and conductor were going to and fro, they had gradually slipped through the doors as they were opened.

Now, one joker in the car in which my friend and her mother were riding with Rice and Roni, thought it funny, too, and said, "I know why they were in the car ahead rather than the car behind us."

"Why?" one rider asked.

"It's obvious," he said, "they wanted to get there before we did, No. 1, and No. 2, I'll bet you Rice said to Roni, 'Honey, let's make our way on up the line to the front engine, take over and hold all of them captive. That way, we will no longer have to stay in a shoe box, and we can stop at one of the fast food places. I'm sure the back door will be open. We can get as much as we want.'"

In any event, mama and daughter never again took Rice and Roni on a train trip.

They Are One Of Us

 As those of us who live in the western mountains of North Carolina well know, groundhogs are as proud and determined in their way as any of the other Appalachian inhabitants.

<Timing>

One old lady who had a reputation for being a cynic felt that her day had not gone just right, and said the vagaries of time were upon her.

"All my life I have given and given, and I have been last in everything. Now why must I be first in death? At least a first for me."

In Order To Collect

The elderly gentleman went to the office and spoke with the lawyer. He wanted help in collecting for some hay he had delivered at the request of a small cattle rancher.

"Well, Mr. Brown, I appreciate your coming in, and I will try to help you. But tell me, when you delivered this hay to him, did you present him with a bill, in writing?

"Indeed I did, sir.

"He said, 'I'll mail you a check.'"

"And he never did?"

"No. And I sent him a second bill, and finally I went to see him about the outstanding amount."

"And what did he say?"

"He said I could go to the devil."

"And what did you do?"

"I came straight to you."

Taxes, Taxes

On the assumption, of course, that I would ascend, not descend, when my time came, I asked the One above if I would have to pay taxes when I arrived.

"No," came the reply. "You are prepaid and will probably be due a refund."

Rest Is Essential

For many, many years I was a court reporter, working in the court system. I took down the witnesses' testimony, arguments by counsel before the court, the judges' charges, depositions and other court-related matters. All verbatim.

You hear human nature wide open, like it probably isn't in any other medium.

Although I never remember such an occasion occurring during any time that I reported for a particular judge, rumors were circulating that one judge in particular had a problem staying awake during some of the trials. It was difficult, some said, to detect this because he would often put his hand up to his forehead, shading his eyes, and you couldn't really tell.

Occasionally, they said, when there was an objection before the Judge to a question by opposing counsel, that counsel would speak out quite emphatically, "Judge I object to the question." Most of the time the increase in voice by counsel for the call for a ruling in regard to the objection would be heard and the judge would rule.

However, on some occasions he was "too far gone" in slumberland, and the bailiff, sensing such condition much sooner than counsel or witness, would simply knock on the banister or railing with his knuckles and heavy ring he wore.

The Judge, apparently tuned in to such a sound, without removing his hand cupping his forehead, would rule: "Sustained" or "Overruled," and the case would continue. The witnesses and audience were unaware of the Judge's problem.

He was a good judge, though, who could cut through the maze of legal jargon quicker than any other I had the opportunity to work with, and he always called it just as he saw it, and, to me, he always called it right.

The Latin Lesson

While scanning through a Latin dictionary, the wife explained that the term "Summum Bonum" meant the chief, the supreme, the highest good, the ultimate goal in living.

"Keep going," said the husband, "so far none of them fits us."

The Jurors Are Right

While traveling through western North Carolina a couple from Pennsylvania was involved in a minor accident with one of the natives. The Pennsylvania couple was sued by the native North Carolinian involved, and the Pennsylvania couple hired a lawyer from the mountain area to represent them.

A jury was chosen, the case was tried, the judge read the charge to the jury, and they were sent to the jury room to deliberate.

Once they had decided to award damages, the glass transom above the wooden door was ajar, and the Judge heard the following:

"Okay, how much are we going to stick this damn Yankee?"

One juror spoke up and said, "Well, it ought to be for the full amount of the policy, and that's $10,000."

The foreman said, "Well, I agree with you that it should be the full amount, but he and his wife did hire one of our lawyers here in the mountains, so let's go easy on him. Why don't we just make it $9,950."

There Is A Point

I can't say that I agree with the Greek philosopher Solon when he said:

"Not that he would be concerned, but no man can be called happy until he is dead."

A Good Deal

When asked why he didn't divorce his wife, the gentleman said, "Because she's neat, that's why:

"She keeps the spices in alphabetical order.

"Things on the refrigerator top shelf are breakfast items.

"The next shelf are the dairy products.

"And the next one, lunch items.

"The bottom one is for dinner items."

 Release

After many years of married life--some more hectic than others--the wife finally decided to proceed with securing a divorce. She contacted a lawyer, necessary papers were filed, and the final day for adjudication arrived.

She appeared with her attorney before the Judge, and the husband showed up without one.

The Judge asked the husband if he was represented, and he said he had not retained an attorney because it would have done no good anyway, plus, it would just cost him money.

And so the wife's attorney began the hearing. She spoke on the terms previously outlined. The Judge listened, after which the attorney offered her client for any questions or comments.

The Judge asked her a few questions and then turned to the defendant husband.

"Do you have any questions you would like to ask the plaintiff or any testimony or statement you'd like to make at this time?"

"No, sir I don't."

And the wife's attorney began to question the husband on certain matters. They had gone on for quite awhile and the husband stopped in the middle of one of his answers and asked, "How much longer is this thing going to last? I want to leave."

The attorney said, "I don't know, but what's your hurry? Why are you in such a big rush?"

"Because I want to get home and play two tapes I bought this morning."

"What tapes did you buy this morning?"

"Well, one of them is 'Free as a Butterfly,' and the other one is 'A Happier Tomorrow.'"

The Real Meaning

One definition of "psychology" is that it is a four-syllable word used to distract attention whenever explaining gets too difficult.

Possible Postponement

Counsel for each side appeared at the designated time and place to begin what was scheduled as a two-day trial. The Judge called both up to the bench for a conference.

"Gentlemen," he said, "I began my vacation early this morning, so I am afraid we're going to have to rush this up or postpone the trial and reset it for another time."

"Your Honor, as counsel for the plaintiff, may I say that this change has come quite unexpectedly, and I can't speak for my colleague here, but we are ready for trial.

"As you may remember, two days were set for this trial, Judge, and it was to begin today."

"I understand," said the Judge.

"Your Honor, as counsel for the defense, I, too, am taken by surprise and quite upset at this last moment's notice.

"May I most respectfully ask how the mix-up occurred, Your Honor?"

The Judge smiled and said, "Well, gentlemen, don't worry. You see, at 7 o'clock this morning I put my wife on a plane for Spain, and she's going to be there for two weeks. So, it's vacation time for me.

"Don't worry. The trial can commence as soon as you two are ready."

Turn About

A cousin of mine was telling me of his experience when a solicitor called right at dinnertime.

"I picked up the phone and said, 'hello.'"

"Is this 480-2391?"

"Yes, it is."

"And are you the occupant of the household?"

"Yes, I am, along with my wife."

"Well, sir, I want you to now that you have been cleared to receive a Gold card."

"Really?"

"Yes, sir, you have."

And then he said he yelled to his wife, "Honey! Honey! Guess what? I'm going to get a Gold card." And he said he acted as if that were the greatest thing in his life.

And she yelled back, "Oh great."

The gentleman said, "And, sir, I think you'll find this one much more generous than the one I presume you presently carry."

After the solicitor proceeded to outline all the benefits of the Gold card over the regular he said, "You do have one, don't you?"

"Listen," said my cousin, "it's right at dinner time. What I would like to do is call you back at your home. Just give me your home phone and as soon as I finish eating I'll ring you back."

"Sir, that's kind of you to make that offer, but I don't like to take calls at my home."

"Neither do I," said my cousin, and he hung up the phone.

He said he has never since been bothered with a call from that particular company.

Bumper Stickers - No. 4

You see more every day. Here are a few that stand out:

This isn't a bumper sticker
I don't like them either

Be kind. I'm old
And want to stay that way

Can we talk
But not with your middle finger

Take me back
To the good old USA

The way to heaven
Is not on my tail

Driver carries no cash
Wife and kids have it all

Doesn't anything good
Ever happen to you?

Married three times
Divorced twice
Stuck all three

Leonard

"Mr. Rhinehart, I am Lieutenant Richards, Rex Richards, with the local police department. I'm calling you from the holding area here at First General Hospital."

"Yes."

"Sir, we picked up a fellow wandering in an open field down south of the city, just off one of the major arteries. He says his name is Leonard Purvis. Do you know a Leonard Purvis?"

"Leonard Purvis. Yes, I do. Did you say you were at a holding area at the hospital?"

"Yes. They have a holding cell for persons who are brought in for observation or may do harm to themselves or to others."

"I wasn't aware of that."

"He says that you are the only person he knows in the state."

"I didn't know he was in Florida. He used to live in New York City. We were in the Service together, stationed at Third Air Force headquarters in Tampa. I haven't seen or heard from him in years."

"He said you two were buddies. Would you come to the hospital, Mr. Rhinehart? He has a problem, and I think your presence might help. Could you come down?"

"Yes, I'll come right now."

"Thank you. We'll be expecting you."

As I rushed to the hospital, I thought of our days at Third Air Force Headquarters. Leonard had just made corporal when he was assigned as typewriter repairman; and although those of us who worked in the Colonel's office were pleased with his mechanical skill, we saw a more interesting side, one we truly loved: his wit.

I arrived at the hospital, parked my car and rushed in.

"Thanks for coming, Mr. Rhinehart. I am not a doctor, but I think Mr. Purvis has an emotional problem. His behavior yesterday was a bit bizarre, and that's why we felt it was better to have him here in the hospital confines.

"He said he flew in three days ago and tried to call you but couldn't get an answer."

"I was out of town for the weekend."

"His actions are unpredictable. Since we picked him up thirty-six hours ago, his behavior has been a bit weird at times, and had we not exercised some firmness, I am afraid there would have been a couple of instances when he might have become violent or hurt himself.

"He said when he was unable to reach you, and didn't have enough money to catch a cab and get a room, he just checked his two bags in one of the airport lockers, put the key in his pocket, and began walking. It was then, he said, he became disoriented and frightened.

"What my fellow officer here and I-- This is Pete MacPherson--"

"Nice to meet you."

"Glad to meet you."

"--would like to do is have you sit here in this room, and we will bring him out. Just sit here. Do nothing and say nothing. Let him make the first move. I don't think he will react violently because he has been given medication by the doctor. So, if you will, just wait here and let's see what happens."

It was easy to recognize Leonard as he walked out

between the two officers. His hair had receded, but he still remained slim and straight.

As they had suggested, I sat perfectly still and said nothing. Leonard made a complete circle around the table, walked straight towards me and stopped directly in front. He did not extend his hand, just stared down at my head.

"I see you still have dandruff," he muttered.

"I didn't realize that, Leonard. How are you doing, buddy?" Then I stood, and he gripped my hand, turned it loose and gave me a friendly pat on the shoulder. I tried again.

"Good to see you again, Leonard. What have you been doing?"

"What's it to you, old friend?"

"No, really, have you been okay?"

"Oh, sure."

Officer Richards asked us to sit.

"Mr. Rhinehart, Mr. Purvis says he left two pieces of luggage in a locker at the airport, and he wants you to pick them up and hold them for him until he can square away. He wants to come home with you, but we think he should not, and the doctor on duty here suggests he rest a bit longer."

Lt. Richards winked.

"Well, I will be happy to pick up his baggage in the airport locker, Lieutenant, but I certainly don't want to get into any trouble. I mean, you picked him up and he is being held here. Wouldn't it be more appropriate if someone from the department did that? I don't mind, you understand, but since this is an unusual situation, I would not want to do anything that would complicate matters."

"Old friend," Leonard butted in, "I would prefer that you pick them up. You can't trust just anybody, you know."

"We have no objection, Mr. Rhinehart."

"You see," Leonard said, "I have two valuable rings in the large suitcase: a 4-carat diamond and a 5-carat opal. That opal is rare. I want you to keep them for me, please."

"Lieutenant, this becomes even more ticklish, now that Leonard has said that."

"Yes. He told us that he had two rings and wanted you to hold them for him."

"Officer, reluctantly, I agree to do this, but I still think someone from your department ought to do it."

"He obviously trusts you, Mr. Rhinehart."

"But, Lieutenant, what if the rings are not in his luggage?"

"They are," Leonard blurted out.

"I mean, you know, you said he has been upset, and maybe this is just..."

"They are in there, friend. Believe me. You know I wouldn't lie. Did I ever lie to you while we were in the Service? I wouldn't, and especially to you."

"All right."

"We would appreciate it," Lieutenant Richards said. "Just pick up the two pieces of luggage and hold them at your house." He handed me the key and said, "I'll be back in touch."

* * *

I arrived at the locker area, found S-542, inserted the key and the door wouldn't open. I tried several times, but without success. I located Security and told her my problem.

"You see," said Security, "the 24 hours has expired. It will take another four quarters. It takes two quarters for each 24 hours."

No problem, I thought.

"Ma'am, since you are with Security, would you stay while I open these two pieces of luggage, and watch as I check the contents?"

"No, that's not my job. I can help in situations like this, where someone has trouble opening a locker, but from then on they are on their own. I'm sorry." She turned and walked away.

I put the two pieces of luggage on the floor. The smaller one contained two pairs of shoes, two sets of underwear, one knit shirt, and a bunch of toilet articles.

The larger piece was bulging. There was a book inside: "Profiles in Courage." Additionally, there were two large, neatly-folded beach towels, three more knitted shirts, three pairs of slacks, and eight pairs of socks, a blue sports jacket, and a white windbreaker.

I dug furiously for another item. It wasn't until I removed each pair of slacks individually that I found a small flat cardboard jewelry-type box between two of the pairs. A rubber band held the lid on. It was stuffed with cotton. I carefully lifted the first layer and found the sparkling diamond and opal rings. Two beautiful pieces. I was relieved.

I drove home and called Lt. Richards.

"Just hold on to the whole works until you hear from me. The doctors have conferred and think that he should spend some time at the South Florida Readjustment Center. Mr. Rhinehart, he is not well. We'll take him up there and he can be further examined by psychiatrists, as well as other doctors. I'm sure he'll get the necessary treatment."

The next morning I took the two rings to a jeweler to learn if they were genuine.

"The diamond is fake," he said. "It's a zircon. The opal is genuine, but there are quite a few imperfections."

I returned home, put them back in the little box, and put it in the large suitcase and stored both pieces of luggage in my closet.

Two days later, the Center called.

75

"Mr. Rhinehart, this is Doctor Wellington."

"Yes, sir."

"Mr. Rhinehart, Mr. Purvis has multiple problems. He really needs several therapies, not just one. He needs treatment."

"I'm glad to hear he's getting help. He was really a great guy in the barracks back in the old days."

"Well, Mr. Rhinehart, I believe you can be of immeasurable assistance in his recovery. You are the only person he talks about. Would it be possible for you to visit him a couple of times a week? This is not going to be an overnight situation."

I visited Leonard as often as my schedule would permit, and found his moods to run the gamut: On one visit he would be calm and friendly; another, irritable; and then the next time, alternately witty and sarcastic.

Weeks passed, and then Leonard began to show improvement. He began to act like his old self, but he did have occasional relapses, and that worried me. After several week I received a phone call.

"Mr. Rhinehart, Dr. Wellington. We think Leonard has made sufficient progress to be able to safely return to New York. I don't think he will be harmful to himself or others. He is on medication, and has been very good about taking it. I think if he continues, there will be no further problem. In fact, at this point we think release will enhance the stabilization of his present status and hasten complete recovery. But he will need to continue on certain medications.

"Will you come here, pick him up and take him to the airport? We have already purchased his ticket to New York."

"Yes, Doctor; and I'm pleased to hear he's doing well."

Although the doctor had said he was sure he was

recovered enough to be released, I continued to wonder if his emotional condition was that stable.

"When should I pick him up?"

"The flight leaves at ll:20 Friday morning.
If you can, come about 9:15. That will give ample time to load and get him there without any sweat. And it will give you two time to talk about the old days.

"You see, Mr. Rhinehart, the idea is that by having him with someone he knows and trusts right at the end of his stay with us, the better the chances for full recovery."

Leonard was delighted to see me. He asked if I had his luggage, and insisted I open the large one so he could check to see if the rings were there. From time to time while he was under treatment, at his request and with permission of the doctors, I had taken over some of his clothing. Now he was finally going to leave what he called the DOG, the Dungeon of Gloom.

On the way we stopped at an ice-cream parlor. The sundae was a favorite of ours while we were in Service, and whenever we were near a place that served them, we stopped in.

"Buddy," he said, "I really appreciate this. It's like old times, isn't it? Some day I will repay you."

"No problem, Leonard. I'm glad to help, and I'm happy you are feeling okay. I hope that you will be able to pick up where you left off."

"Don't worry about me. You did put the two rings back in the suitcase, didn't you?"

"Yes. Remember, you checked them just before we left the DOG."

"Right. Doesn't hurt to see if you're still on the ball."

We finished eating and drove to the airport, removed the luggage from the car and walked up near the check-in counter. Leonard suddenly stopped, unzipped the larger piece of luggage and took out "Profiles in Courage," zipped it back up and put the luggage on the check-in platform. He clutched the book as if he were afraid someone was going to grab it.

The agent validated his ticket, and we walked to the boarding area and waited.

"Flight 304 is now ready for boarding at Gate 5."

Leonard sat perfectly still.

"That's your flight," I said.

He said, "I know. There's no rush. Let the commoners get settled in."

Others boarded, but he just sat. "Leonard, you had better board; they just made the final call."

"I will," he said, "but first I want you to have this."

He opened to the inside front cover of "Profiles in Courage", scribbled a couple of short sentences, signed his name beneath, and then stood as he handed it to me.

"I wrote that book," he said. "Enjoy it."

"I'm sure I will, Leonard."

"I have also written others. I wrote 'You Can't Go Home Again' and 'Gone With the Wind.' And not long ago I wrote a sequel to that one. I titled it 'Scarlett.' I will bring you a copy of each on my next visit. I'll autograph them, too."

"That will be great, Leonard. You know I have always enjoyed reading, and it will be a special treat, especially when I know the author."

Leonard drew himself up tall, clicked his heels together, came to attention, looked me straight in the eye as he gave a precise salute, and then executed a firm about-face and marched in perfect cadence down the jetway entrance.

Congratulations

The employer welcomed the employee back after returning from her honeymoon.

She thanked her boss and then asked, "Now that I'm married and want to begin a family, sir, do you think that you could give me a raise?"

"Well, now," he said, "I'm sorry, but you know, Melissa, we are not responsible for accidents that occur outside the workplace."

The Unread Judge

It was a small country town where the young man was brought before the local magistrate for being drunk and disorderly.

"Robert, do you have anything to say why sentence should not be pronounced?"

"Yes, I do, Judge. 'Man's inhumanity to man makes countless thousands mourn,'" he began. "I am not so debased as Poe, so profligate as Byron, so ungrateful as Keats, so intemperate as Burns, so timid as Tennyson, so vulgar as Shakespeare, so--"

The Judge interrupted. "That'll do. I'm going to sentence you to ten days.

"And, Officer, take down that list of names he just mentioned and round them up. I think they are as bad as he is."

Different? What Difference?

Loretta and Olga were elderly neighbors and their husbands, though friendly to one another, had little in common. John was the physical type and Mercer the brainy type. Some said that both John and Loretta were aging more "upstairs" than each of their body's showed.

Routinely, John would take his morning walk, passing Olga and Mercer's home. On one occasion when the two ladies were having coffee at Olga's house, John passed, but this time was walking backwards, albeit at a slightly slower pace. He was swinging his arms, and moving with the typical vigor so many elder people use..

"Loretta," Olga asked, "I see John's on his morning walk again, but look, it's not the same. He's walking--"

"Oh," interrupted Loretta, "that's John for you. He's crazy about that red sweater and wears it every chance he gets."

Maybe

Isn't a budget just a gimmick or method to make us worry before we spend instead of afterwards?

Why Try?

If I sit backwards
I don't see frontwards.
If I sit frontwards,
I don't see backwards.
If I sit sideways
It brings on a daze.

Why not become a slouch,
Lie prone upon the couch.
Then wait for him or her
Before you try to stir.

Be not disturbed at age,
Just try to be a sage.
This life is meant for Joy,
Even though we use a ploy.

Try

Don't forget the peace of mind

That comes from the Inner Source.

From birth until we die

We cultivate its very death.

It matters not how we reach the goal

At long as we've not hurt the soul.

The Real Reason

Maybe it is true what they said about George Washington and the cherry tree, and the fact that he could not tell a lie. But I suspect another reason he couldn't is because at that time they didn't have primaries.

Could Be

The traveler stopped along the country road to ask directions from the farmer plowing his field. After receiving the directions, they began talking about the farmer's horse.

"He's a beautiful specimen," said the traveler. "Do you plow him all day?"

"Oh, yes," said the farmer.

"And doesn't he get tired?"

"No," the farmer said. "You see, horses are bred so that their front legs are shorter than their hind legs, and as a result they think they are walking downhill all the time."

Overuse

Don't you think we overuse
The words "if" and "but"?
I sometimes think
If they were candy and nuts,
We could have Christmas every day.

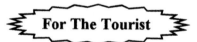

For The Tourist

While in Italy one of the more friendly locals, who spoke excellent English, was explaining to the tourist the history of his town. And then he added, "Here in Italy, we have an old traditional saying, that if you kiss a new baby on the lips, it will be a good singer; on the hands, it will be a good pianist, and on the feet, a good dancer."

"I see," said the tourist. "And which one of those are you?"

The local answered, "Well, I am not any of those, but I am a good chairman."

Help Me

Is it correct that a pediatrician is a doctor with little patients?

Take Your Choice

A regular street sign posted just outside the community cemetery read:

"One Way - Do Not Enter." Across the street was the funeral home with its sign that read:
"Try Our Lay-Away Plan."

Bumper Stickers - No. 5

Looking for the right man?
I ain't it.

Pauline wouldn't marry me
So I married her sister

The Lord giveth
And the Lord taketh away
So does the mortgage company

I like sweet potatoes, sweet peas
And sweet women

Take advantage of your youth
Old age ain't so hot

Honk if you're not available
Go ahead - everybody else does

Don't pass - there's a cop ahead

Keep speeding
The cemetery isn't yet full

Take my woman, take my liquor
But leave my dog, his name is Flicker

I'm sorry
It won't go any faster

Think You Have It Bad Now

Take a look at the Notice to Employees' work rules back in 1852.

These were regulations for a Burnley cotton mill office during that time, as published in Vol. 164 of the 1981 Farmers' Almanac:

1. Godliness, cleanliness and punctuality are the necessities of a good business.

2. This firm has reduced the hours of work, and the

clerical staff will now only have to be present between the hours of 7:00 a.m. and 6:00 p.m. on weekdays.

3. Daily prayers will be held each morning in the main office. The clerical staff will be present.

4. Clothing must be of a sober nature. The clerical staff will not disport themselves in raiment of bright colours, nor will they wear hose, unless in good repair.

5. Overshoes and top-coats may not be worn in the office, but neck scarves and headwear may be worn in inclement weather.

6. A stove is provided for the benefit of the clerical staff. Coal and wood must be kept in the locker. It is recommended that each member of the clerical staff bring four pounds of coal each day during cold weather.

7. No member of the clerical staff may leave the room without permission from Mr. Rogers. The calls of nature are permitted and clerical staff may use the garden below the second gate. This area must be kept in good order.

8. No talking is allowed during business hours.

9. The craving of tobacco, wines or spirits is a human weakness and, as such, is forbidden to all members of the clerical staff.

10. Now that the hours of business have been drastically reduced, the partaking of food is allowed between 11:30 a.m. and noon, but work will not, on any account, cease.

11. Members of the clerical staff will provide their own pens. A new sharpener is available, on application to Mr. Rogers.

12. Mr. Rogers will nominate a senior clerk to be responsible for the cleanliness of the main office and the private office, and all boys and juniors will report to him 40 minutes before prayers, and will remain after closing hours for similar work. Brushes, brooms, scrubbers and soap are provided by the owners.

(The owners recognize the generosity of the new Labour Laws, but will expect a great rise in output of work to compensate for these near utopian conditions.)

Whew! That's a lot to swallow, but then so is the situation today.

When asked if he knew why at church weddings the bride and groom always walked up to the altar slowly as opposed to their normal everyday gait, the fellow replied, "Well, I can't say that I do know, but it seems to me like it's because they're not quite sure they want to take that final step."

"I read the other day, John, that the Government wants to start taxing the churches. Did you hear anything about that?"

"No, I didn't, but it wouldn't surprise me. I guess they want to get their share of the Almighty dollar."

On Notice

I'll tell you one thing: Discovering that your driver's license has expired will very quickly improve your driving habits.

Justice?

Here's to love,

Oh, ain't it grand.

I just got rid of a no-count man.

I laughed and laughed

At the Court's decision.

They give him the children

And they won't even his'n.

Really?

There are ways of being frank, but the following carries it a little too far:

"Oh, I shouldn't make such a pig of myself?"

"Why not?" asked the companion. "I don't see anything wrong with self-improvement."

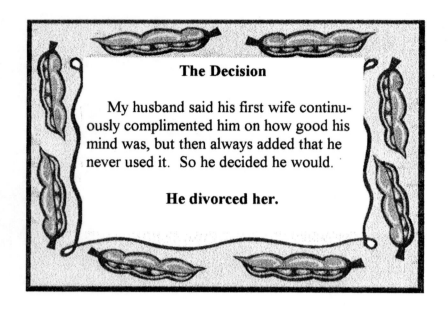

The Decision

My husband said his first wife continuously complimented him on how good his mind was, but then always added that he never used it. So he decided he would.

He divorced her.

Humorous Tidbits

A delightful Jonesborough, Tennessee woman, along in years, has not lost her zest for life and great sense of humor. While autographing books in that area, she came by, looked through some of the pages of the first humor book and said, "I'll give you a few, if you like."

"Fine," I said, "shoot."

And then she took off:

"You heard about the man who said he wouldn't come back to church anymore because they stopped bringing covered dishes. He said he always came for a wing and a prayer."

"And the thoughtlessly unkind woman that stepped inside the church to attend the wedding, and the usher, quite obviously bowlegged, asked, 'Ma'am, are you a relative or friend of the bride or the groom?'

'The groom,' she said.

'Just walk this way.'

'I'll try,' she said."

And then, without a break or notes, the grand lady continued her recitations:

"You heard about the librarian that ordered alphabet soup for lunch, but said she would never do it again. And when asked why, she said, 'because it takes so long to get through the alphabet.'"

"And the farmer that fed his sheep iron pills because his wife wanted some steel wool.

"When the Scotchman came over and applied for a police job, he was being interviewed by the officer in command.

'How would you handle a situation such as a 'crowd riot?'"

"'Oh,' said the Scotchman, 'I guess I would pass the hat.'"

"And then there was the fanatical crossword puzzle worker who died. They thought it would be appropriate to do something to remember him by, so they buried him six down and three across."

And this charming lady never stopped.

"The doctor fell in the well and was moaning and

groaning. He was finally pulled out, so now he only tends the sick and leaves the well alone.

"The young fellow went to the psychiatrist complaining that every time he put his hat on he heard music playing.

"The doctor said, 'Let me have your hat.'

"The young man handed the hat to the doctor, and the doctor removed the headband, handed it back to the guy and said, 'Put the hat on now and let's see if you hear music.'

"The guy put the hat on, waited a few seconds, and said, 'No, I don't. What did you do, Doctor?'

"'I removed the band.'"

And then she ended with a pretty clever one: "I was born on soil so poor that my dog had to lean up against a fence to grow a bark."

It was a genuine delight to see this 80-plus-year-old woman so full of humor.

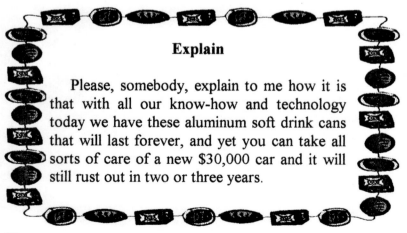

Explain

Please, somebody, explain to me how it is that with all our know-how and technology today we have these aluminum soft drink cans that will last forever, and yet you can take all sorts of care of a new $30,000 car and it will still rust out in two or three years.

Mostly True

I totally agree with the anonymous writer who said that a politician is a man who thinks twice before saying positively nothing, or is it nothing positively.

Speed

A friend of mine sent this little bovine piece of humor:

A farmer was helping one of his cows to birth the calf, and it required a lot of pulling on the rear legs of the calf. When he had finished, he noticed that his small son had been watching. Now's the time for a little sex education for my son, he thought.

"So what do you think of that?" he asked the young boy.

"Well, how fast was that calf going when it hit the cow?" the young fellow asked.

Selfishness

The teacher, speaking to her third grade class, was explaining how rewarding it is to help others, to think of others first, and in general to be willing to give of yourself until it hurts or be willing to do without something that you not only wanted, but in fact something you needed.

"Ralph," she asked, "can you give me an example of a time when you go without something you really need?"

"Yes, ma'am. There are times when I go without a bath when I really need one."

Careful About The Advice

The wife was sitting at the sewing machine hemming a skirt when the husband walked in. He walked over, pulled up a chair and sat beside her.

"Look out," he said, "you're zipping along too fast. The first thing you know-- Watch out, you're going to sew the wrong seam there. Are you sure you're stitching that down the way it should be? Look at the corner there."

The wife looked up and asked, "Robert, what is wrong with you? Don't you know I've been sewing since way before our marriage, and that was many years ago."

"I know you have, but I just thought you might like some help from me. After all, I was driving way before we were married, and you still help me drive the car."

Observations

(Check-in Counter Waiting Area No. 4 - Los Angeles airport)

HE

The Weasel Wimp
The Bearded Weirdy
The Cardiovascular Candidate
Death perambulating unassisted
The Towering Torso minus Mental Baggage
Hairy-Scary
Warmup suits on parade

The dungaree gent, much too bent
American bulk has always been "in"; now they've added
　　sweaters

SHE

The calorie flood victim
Sculptured ungliness enveloped in variegated yarn
Human Faces: Mobile Art Deco
Mother Haggard and her four misfits
Intransit passengers: Gerbils *sans* the wheel
The corduroy doll sporting acne makeup
Washed straight hair and rosy cheeks perched atop loosely
　　structured fat
Wholesome bosoms blossoming under bulk
The paisley scarf enjoying a bosom rest
The walking earring tree
The leotard tarts with generous hearts

ITS

Prance Valiant and the off-duty waiter who dares to cater

For Lovers

When it comes to a twinkle in the eye, I wonder if it would
make any difference to lovers if they realized that the
twinkling in the sky does not originate with the star itself; it is
just an atmospheric illusion.

New Discovery

And while on the romantic theme, you might be interested to know that they have now discovered that the mating call for the Mediterranean fruit fly has exactly the same frequency as the lower F sharp on the harmonica.

Does this mean that we will be seeing more musicians than usual, and especially those who play the harmonica?

Listen

If you really want to be grateful, don't fret about all the things you want but don't get; instead, be thankful for all the things that you don't get that you don't want.

Don't Believe

Is there any wonder there are so many divorces these days? With all our technology and automation, life has been made so easy that women *can* do it all.

The Illnesses

There are many from head to toe, and a doctor for each.
    If it's the feet, see the podiatrist. He counts to see
    if there are five toes on each, a heel and a ball beneath.
Now if it's the veins above or in the legs,
    we see a "special" specialist.
He looks, gently caresses.
    "Oh, yes, these are spider veins,
    but tests show others present, too,
    though deeper and more serious."

Now if the kneecap is not on just right,
    misplaced by accident or wear and tear,
    we see the orthopedist.
    She (or he) is the expert in crepitation,
    crack, snap and pop. But inactivity, pins
    and glue will help.

And what about the hip?
    We can't overlook this crippling malady
    which affects so many.
    Steel rods, pins and careful exercise
    and walking rights the problem now and then.

The stomach is not forgotten.
    The gastroenterologist reaches to unknown
    depths to repair, and opens with his tiny

instrument, encompassing a light. Here
he discovers a cornucopia of conflicts: scar
tissue, polyps, ulcers, benign tumors, or maybe
not benign.

We move to the chest.
Here comes the pulmonary expert.
He breathes and asks you to--deeply.
He looks at your lungs, finds beehives of
honeycomb filled with years of abuse.
Today is the beginning for some, for others
a continuing down the path of a slow and
painful death.

Now it's the face we entrust to the dermatologist.
He rids us from acne in youth, eradicates the
skin cancers caused from over-exposure to
the sun and excessive pride.

Life's motor, the heart, we give to the cardiologist.
He knows we have one because it's taught
in first-year medical school. And when it ticks
not in synch, he can tell. If the arteries,
particularly the large ones, become clogged
or fall down on the job, he knows what to do.

It's now the brain.
We know much about its functions and roadmap"
vessels, veins and connecting tissues. The nerves
help us maneuver, and the petuitary gland stands
guard and is the command post. Keep the brain
in shape and you will go a long way toward
mental and physical well-being.

Orthopedics: Our bones need some help, and the
　　orthopedist is there with all his might.

Neurologist: There are many nerves in our body,
　　and these professionals help us keep them
　　sending messages to the brain.

Psychiatrist: Many need to tell their tales to someone
　　who can accept them for what they really are.
　　These professionals are good listeners, too.
　　　　　　　(It's part of their training.)

Pscyhologist: The counsel is often helpful for many in
　　today's world or turmoil.

Rheumatoidologist: Joints are often greased by
　　these professionals, who use salves,
　　heat, pills or liquid medication.

Sexologist: Perhaps the most satisfying professional
　　of all, when the recommended services are
　　sensibly and patiently utilized. It is a real
　　commitment to healthy living.

So, today it matters not the problem, there are answers in
part, in whole, or not at all.

Subject

The outdoor signboard in front of the church, along with the regular announcements re time, et cetera, carried the following:

Evening Subject:
"What is Hell like?"
Come and hear our organist.

Repair or Relief

Not too many years ago, in a small town in North Florida, one of the radiator repair shops once had a large sign on the side of their building which read:
The best place in town to take a leak

(I'm told it was a great relief to many because they did excellent work.)

Obey

A friend swears someone told him about the talking scales. He said there was one gentleman, considerably overweight, who got on and immediately heard them say:: "One at a time, please."

Bumper Stickers - No. 6

Heaven has to be better
But I can't play the harp

I can't believe
What you're now thinking

If you think I'm old
Wait 'til YOU get there

Despite what you may think
I'm still a good person

Old people wouldn't be so bad
If they didn't act their age

If I'm wrong
Just be patient

Oh? Go ahead, laugh
But I paid cash for mine

Must She?

Some people really are sourpusses, but I recently saw one walking by, as I sat signing books in a mall, that really took the cake. I think if she ever smiled it had to have been while she was in the womb.

Believe It Or Not

Maybe you've heard about the youngster in school who, when asked about his background said, "Well, I'm really a half-breed."

"Oh," said the teacher, "what do you mean?"

"You see, my father is a man and my mother is a woman."

The Reason

The steak lover called the waiter over, pointed to the steak the waiter had just served him and said, "What in the world is this?"

The waiter replied, "Well, sir, it's your steak. I believe you ordered it medium rare."

"That's right, I did," said the customer, "but look--it isn't half as large as the one I ordered last night when I was in here, and I ordered the very same thing. Why is that?"

"Where did you sit last night, sir?" the waiter asked.

"Right over there by that row of windows."

"Ah, that explains it," said the waiter. "When people sit by the window we give them bigger helpings. It's our best advertisement."

* * *

The feeling of the earth is nothing more than the urge to follow nature through its intended course.

No Pain

It's a little much to ask us to believe that they gave a patient a local anesthetic because they couldn't afford the imported stuff.

Jilted

Two married men were out on the golf course, and while waiting to play through they were talking about marriage in general.

"Tell me," said George to his playing partner, "have you ever been disappointed in love?"

"Yes, I have," said the other. "You see, the first one jilted me and the second one didn't."

Planting

No home construction goes perfectly, and my own was no exception. There are many incidents that occurred throughout that I could relate, but one stands out, perhaps because it is so amusing.

Three young men among the work crew were punctual, did excellent work, were interesting to talk to, and occasionally showed signs of good humor.

They had been working very hard this one day, and near the end told the foreman on the job that they would not be back the next day.

"Why?" asked the foreman, "We've got a lot more work to do here, many more days. Why are you taking off?"

"We've got to get our taters in the ground. The time is right for it."

"My god," said the foreman, "can't you plant them on Saturday?"

"No, we can't do it then; the signs are wrong."

"Well, look," said the foreman, "do you realize that with the money you could make working tomorrow--just one day-- you would be able to buy all the potatoes you will eat for the whole year?"

"That's not the point," said one of the guys. "You gotta do it yourself and then let nature take its course."

"Okay," said the foreman, "we'll see you the day after tomorrow. And good luck with your potatoes."

 Diamonds Can Be Your Best Friend

My offices were located in a large office building in downtown Miami. Rest rooms were on each floor, and those who rented offices in the building had their own key to open the door.

On one occasion I stopped to insert my key and happened to glanced down toward the floor. There, right in front of me, was a pair of sparkling diamond earrings.

I inserted the key, opened the door, and with my foot pushed them inside, and closed the door behind me.

Just as I reached down to pick them up another occupant came in. I showed them to him. He said they looked real.

That evening I took them home and several friends also

said they thought they were real. The following morning I went directly to the jeweler located in my office building and asked him if he would appraise them.

"Let me see a moment," he said. He held them close to his eye and said, "I will appraise them if you want, but you will be just wasting your money because I can tell from looking at them with my naked eye that they are not diamonds; they are backed glass cut to look like diamonds."

It was then I inquired of the manager of the building as to whether anyone had reported lost earrings. None had, but I left them with him for weeks and no one claimed them. He called and told me to pick them up. I did, and they are to this day in my cuff link box.

Oddly enough, my "diamonds" have not increased in value.

"A" Average All The Way

The sixteen-year-old boy was popular in school. His grades were all A's and he excelled in sports, especially soccer. It was his life. His father was behind him a hundred percent, taking him to all practice sessions, as he progressed to state games and state team practice.

He became known throughout the state and then the National teams were becoming interested in his capabilities and unique talent in soccer.

On one occasion father and son got up at 4:30 in the morning to venture over to the opposite side of the state for an exhibition game.

They had been on the road for just a short period, and were barreling along the Interstate. The son, still sleepy-eyed,

103

was half listening while the father told of how proud he was of his abilities, and how great it was that he loved his sport and was so dedicated to soccer.

He said, "Son, you are damn good at it, and you know it. Let's face it, you're smart."

The son quickly shot back, "Well, if I'm so smart, Dad, why are all my friends asleep at this time of the day?"

Menglish And Femglish

An article from an excellent writers' newsletter spoke of the sexes finding "Menglish" and "Femglish" incompatible. Men, the article read, are really from another continent where they speak a form of English called Menglish, and women, on the other hand, being from celestial pedestals, speak Femglish. And it is for this reason--and not surprising--that often when the male is speaking Menglish, he is often not understood by the Femglish speaker. The article cited many humorous examples, one of which is listed here:

"Take a break, honey, you're working too hard," really means, "I can't hear the game over the vacuum cleaner."

It May Be Worth It

Many writers probably think Jawaharial Nehru, a former prime minister of India, and once imprisoned, had a valid point, when he said:

"All my major works have been written in prison. I would recommend prison not only to aspiring writers but to aspiring politicians, too."

I'm willing to let the politicians try it first, and with no time limit on their prison stay.

Croquet

These days you don't hear much about croquet being played here in the United State. This game is played by driving wooden balls through a series of wire arches by means of a long-handled mallet. (Is polo an offshoot from croquet?).

This is not an expensive game to play, but I suggest another oldtimer that requires hardly any outlay, and that is the toe-bag races.

Years ago at some of the family gatherings, the women and men would often take the large toe-bags that are made from cloth or hemp--the kind of bag that peanuts, fertilizer and feed were stored in olden days. You need not wear any particular type clothing. It does help, though, to be bare-footed, although not a requirement. Each player steps inside one of the bags and they line up abreast of one another, pulling the bag up as far as the waist, if it is that long. All begin "racing" as fast as they can toward a designated site as the goal to reach. They must never remove themselves from the toe-bag, just keep "stumbling" along with that confinement. The first one reaching the site wins, and so on.

There were occasions when several of the women would play a match by themselves, as would the men, and then the winner of each gender would race, to see who could win.

This sport is fun and harmless. Children are good at it.

Lessie The Leech

Now, with her money she's reasonably generous
It's her labor she's stingy about.
And one can't accuse her of lack of generosity
When it comes to laziness, for it abounds.

She sits and smokes,
Eats and dotes--it doesn't matter on what;
Offering gab galore
Until you must ignore,

For nothing is so agitating
As a moocher in style
That comes on today
And all the while.

If you don't watch her, too,
She'll tipple the bottle
'Til her lips become loose
And her tongue quite thick.

They'll each stumble over the other
and it will surely make you sick.

But Lessie the Leech
Will always be Lessie
And certainly a leech
As she maneuvers, connives,

And daily transports
Her body and appetite--
You can bet on that--
To other food ports.

That Special Seat

I particularly like the story about the two girls in their late teens or early twenties who boarded the crowded subway, and one of them, trying to impress the other, said in a low voice, "Watch me. I am going to try to embarrass one of those men over there into giving up his seat."

She edged her way through to one unsuspecting middle-aged fellow and looked him straight in the eye and said, "Oh, Mr. Gregory, I never expected to see you on this subway, but I'm glad. It has been so long I hardly recognized you."

The quiet gentleman knew he was getting the fast shuffle.

He looked up at her and as he began to rise said, "Oh, please do sit down, Juanita. It isn't often I see you except on washday. And by the way, don't deliver it until Friday; my wife is going to the District Attorney's office to see if she can get your husband out of jail."

Bare Facts

Many of us grew up in the country without indoor plumbing, and the outside "privy" was a part of that existence. Although I have heard it referred to as many things, one lady stepped up at a book signing, and in the course of the conversation mentioned that she was raised on a farm. She said--and I use her words--"I was raised out on a farm where we had a "Path to the Bath.""

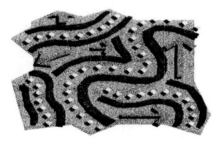

The First Time

Marvalena Panky had been in the mountains only two weeks when she met Bossy Spence. Her local friends said he was a jolly sort, always full of surprises. She wondered whether their introduction two days earlier at the pig-picking picnic would lead to more than just the usual exchange of mountain howdy-do's and small talk.

"Jewel," Marvalena asked, "do you think he was interested in me?"

"Marvalena, that man is interested in any young woman-- and you're a young woman, aren't you?"

"Yes, I am. We did talk for a short spell, but he didn't really give me the impression that he was too interested. I remember he said that he could show me many of the places here in the mountains."

"Well, don't you consider that interest?"

"In a way, yes. I remember he said, 'When God created the universe, he reserved certain sections of the country for people like me and other good ole country boys. And, Marvalena, this is one of them places.'

"Then he sort of hesitated, and with a knowing smile said, 'God thought it would be a good place for outsiders like you to visit, too.'

"You see, Jewel, he sort of raised his voice when he said, 'outside,' so I don't know. There was kind of a 'You're not one of us' tone in his voice, but then I may just be imagining things."

"Oh, don't pay any attention to that," Jewel said. "He loves to talk, never met a stranger in his life. And while some haven't had the best education up here in what some of the outsiders call 'backwoods mountains,' his heart is in the right place. I'll bet you, Marvalena, he'll be calling you before long. He knows my number; I've known him for years."

It was three days later that the phone rang late in the evening. Jewel answered and said, "Marvalena, it's for you. He says he doesn't want to speak to me, not Jewel Sprinkle, just to you, Marvalena Panky. But he's always carrying on like that."

"Hello."

"Aren't you the sweet thang I met at the picnic a few days back?"

"I'm Marvalena Panky, if that's who you're asking for."

"You're right. This is Bossy Spence. Do you remember me?"

"Yes, I do. You're calling a bit late, aren't you? It's almost midnight."

"Well, Marvalena, when a man has thoughts like I have right now, he really don't think about the clock. Do you mind talking?"

"Oh, no, not really."

"Well, I've known Jewel for nigh on since we were born. We were in school in the first grade, and then she passed me up a couple of times before I graduated. I had to repeat the fourth and sixth grades. She knows I'm harmless as a de-fanged snake."

For a moment, Marvalena began to wonder why he had really called, and then she found out.

"Marvalena, I want to take you to see a place that you've never seen before. Nowhere in this United States is there anything like what I will show you. It will be the first time you will have ever seen something like it. I think the experience will leave you not believing what you see. How about it?"

"Just a minutes, Bossy."

Marvalena turned to Jewel and repeated, in a low whisper, what Bossy had said.

"Go ahead and go," Jewel said. "He's not a bad man, just friendly and interested in women. Some say only for friendship. I know he never married, but that don't mean nothing these days."

Marvalena turned back to the phone. "Well, yes, Bossy, I'll go with you. What is this sight or thing you'll take me to that will leave me so awed?"

"Now what was that word you used?"

"I said what is this sight or thing you'll take me to that will leave me so awed?"

"Never mind, sweet thang. Just trust me. You will have lots to tell the folks farther down south when you return from up here in these mountains."

It was two days later that Bossy picked Marvalena up right after lunch and drove through two small towns, down through a valley, and then he stopped on the side of the road.

"Take a look up, will you, Marvalena? Don't them mountains get to you? They's the best piece of handiwork God ever made, except woman. When he tackled that project he had many failures, but for the most part he done a great job, many masterpieces, and you are one of them masterpieces, Marvalena.

"But, Marvalena, don't you think there is something special and spiritual about these mountains? Just look. They are majestic. The word is kind of hard for me to say. I can't say some of them big words, but I know what they mean."

"Bossy, they are beautiful, but you said that you were going to take me some place and show me a sight I had never seen--that it would be a first for me."

"That's right, and I am. We ain't there yet. It's up the road apiece."

Bossy drove another mile or so, came to a very sharp curve, and situated on a hill was a tiny white church at the edge of an old cemetery.

"Come with me," he said. They got out of the car, walked up the short pathway to the church entrance. Looking toward the church, he said, "We'll go in there later. Come this way."

Bossy took her hand, they zigzagged through the cemetery graveyard, and came upon one area with older tombstones, crudely hewn. He stopped, turned to Marvalena and said, "Do you remember the 'Frankie and Johnny' story many years ago, the story about the woman here in the mountains that killed her husband and chopped him into pieces?"

"Yes, I do. They hanged her. And there was a song, 'Frankie and Johnny Were Sweethearts.' There is a poem; I've read about it, too. Oh, yes, I remember it."

"Well," said Bossy, "you see that tombstone there?"

"Yes. Is that where he is buried?"

"Yes, it is. And you see this tombstone next to it?"

"Right. Who's buried there?"

"He's also buried there."

"What? Two places? I don't understand."

"And you see this one next to the second one?"

"Bossy, don't be ridiculous. Do you expect me to believe this?"

"Well, you should because it is a fact. Do you remember when I told you, Marvalena, that I would take you to a sight you'd never seen, and show you something you would see for the first time?"

"Yes, I do. But what is it all about?"

"When Frankie murdered Johnny and then chopped him up, she hid pieces in various places. As the relatives and authorities searched, they found pieces of his body at different times. And when they gathered the parts they buried them.

"You see, in those days it was not acceptable to open or dig into the first grave. And because of this, they buried the parts in three different graves, as the body parts were found."

"I just can't believe it," said Marvalena. "You are right, this is the first time I have ever seen anything like this."

"I told you it would be a 'first time' for you.

"Now, Marvalena, let's go back there and look at the inside of the church, and then go back and I will tell Jewel what we've done. I didn't even tell her what I was going to do."

Bossy and Marvalena meandered throughout the old church, looking at the pictures hung on the wall and reading various pieces about the murder.

They got in the car and drove back to Jewel's place. And as Marvalena got out of the car and began walking up the steps, Jewel opened the door and Marvalena said, "Jewel, that's the first time I've seen a body buried in three grave plots. Whew! That's scary."

"Ain't that something," said Jewel.

Bossy said, "Well, there ain't none of us knows what will happen to us tomorrow, so we better be ready, but I sure hope I don't get chopped up. You wouldn't do that, would you, you sweet thang?"

A Plug Doesn't Hurt

Authors have their ego--at least most of them--and when praise comes their way, they are always delighted. It is customary for most book stores to announce the presence of authors when they are on the premises signing, but one announcer was particularly specific in this duty:

"Good afternoon, shoppers. We thank you for coming in. This afternoon we are fortunate to have two authors, Taylor Reese and Jack Pyle, with us. Come over and meet these wonderful writers. You will find them at their table located in the Features area right next to Self-Help."

When You're 18

I doubt there are many in our country today who would agree with a former friend of mine, now deceased, who had had it "up to here" with kids. When I tried to explain to him that "kids will be kids," and that he, too, was once one, it didn't seem to faze him, at least not outwardly.

He may have been joking--at least I hope so--when he did finally comment, "You know, sometimes I'm of the opinion that when kids are born they ought to be taken outside, planted, watered and fed, and let them grow.

"And when they reach the age of 18, dig them up and let them go."

I might add, although he had a lovely wife, they never had any children, and it was probably by design.

Air Unfiltered

I can't remember who said it, but it has never been more true than it is today, and it is to this effect: "It has often been noted that more speeches by more people from the government have been delivered more solemnly, listened to more patiently, absorbed more quietly and forgotten more promptly than any form, of human discourse."

How true, how true.

Just A Trip

The elderly but eloquent speaker stood before a large crowd of people and suggested that if they were going to speak before a group, it would be a good idea to keep in mind three things. "They are," he said: 'How to diet,' 'How to improve your sex life,' and 'How to make money.'"

And then he continued. "If you look at me and take a look at the jowls and portly exposure, I obviously don't know a doggone thing about diet.

"Now as to how to improve your sex life, well, the first years were very good to me and I participated fully. And today I still have the same agility, the strength, the virility, however, I am in a different capacity: Today I am a consultant."

And then he proceeded to speak on the third, "How to make money," explaining the advantages of government savings bonds.

An Effort

The rather independent fellow applied for a position with a well-known company. "What can you do?" inquired the interviewer.

"Well, the truth be known, sir, not much. I guess you could actually say, nothing."

"I'm sorry to hear that because you look like a pretty nice fellow, but I'm afraid we won't be able to help you. You see, we don't have any executive level openings at the moment."

No Sleep

And then there was the lady who complained to the doctor that she had been unable to sleep since her husband divorced her.

"I understand," said the doctor. "That's a typical anxiety response."

"No, no, I don't think it is, Doctor. I think it's more than that. You see, he took the bed with him."

Jail

The story goes that in a rural area of one of the Carolina mountains an elderly woman, nearly a hundred, began to act bizarre, and the family became concerned.

As weeks went by she became more unpredictable in her actions. The family decided that she probably would be better off at the mental institution quite a few miles away.

So the sheriff came out and talked to her. He thought she might resist, but she calmly climbed in the car. He closed the door and drove off.

As they were traveling down the road things were going all right, but the sheriff heard her muttering, and so he listened and heard her mumbling something about "boy." It sounded like, "Boy, I sure hope them young'uns don't turn that stove oven on."

"And why do you hope they don't turn the stove oven on?" he asked.

"'Cause I got a box of 12-gauge shotgun shells in there."

"Why in the world would you put them in there?"

"Because my grandson is adrinking; and, Sheriff, you know how his temper is when he takes to drinking."

The sheriff said, "I'll tell you what I'm going to do. I'm going to take you back home so you can get them cartridges out of the oven. Do you realize that somebody could get their head blown off?"

The old lady said nothing. He turned the car around, drove back and pulled up to the house. She got out and went in. It was only a couple of minutes before she came back out on the porch holding a double-barreled 12-gauge shotgun in her hands.

"Sheriff," she said, "I ain't got a thing agin you, but I've changed my mind about going to that crazy house."

It didn't take the sheriff long to figure out that he had been tricked, and he thought to himself, "Anybody smart enough to think that one up don't need to go to that place. I probably need to be there myself."

A Special Breakfast

While attending business college in Norfolk, Virginia I stayed in two different places: one a large old home on Freemason Street, where the elderly owner/landlady rented out rooms. Money was scarce, and I began staying there with the understanding that I would get room and board, and sleep on the hall couch at night. I was to greet any late-comers and show them to their room. I was also expected to stoke the furnace in the early morning hours, and then have breakfast with her before school.

The arrangement lasted only a few weeks, and the departure was a friendly one. She said she couldn't afford to feed me breakfast (her servings were not sufficient for a teenager to exist anyway), and at night she ordered from a nearby restaurant. That also was too expensive, she said. So I would have to look for another place.

I began looking at the ads, but it was through one of my paternal aunts--a woman with a heart of gold--that I got to go on an interview. My aunt agreed to go along, to ask questions of the person who had put the ad in, to see if they were willing to give me room and board for whatever services it was they wanted.

When we arrived at the private residence, it turned out to be rented by a naval commander, his wife and young son, not more than two years old. I would go to college during the day and then be at home at night to baby-sit when the naval commander and his wife were out entertaining or being entertained.

At first the wife was a bit hesitant. She said she had anticipated that it would be a girl applying for the job, and

118

that she didn't know whether I could change diapers and all of that stuff like most girls knew. Further, she said she didn't know how her husband would feel about having a young boy there to take care of the child when they were out at night.

My aunt explained that I had two younger brothers and had had ample experience at changing diapers and, in general, looking over the younger two.

The wife still hesitated, and my aunt said, "Listen, may I suggest this: Why don't you call your husband and tell him about us, and while you do that, talk it over, my nephew and I will take a walk around the block."

"A good idea," the wife said, and so we left the house and began walking around the neighborhood.

My aunt, always the "solutioner" in times of need, said to me, "You know, you never have to worry about him crying or being upset, because with a name like they have, if you just repeat it a few times, with a little emphasis, it will make him stop crying, and he will laugh."

"I hope you're right," I said.

"You know he will," she said, "with a name like 'Hogebum,' he's bound to be amused, so you don't have to worry."

We returned from our walk and the wife met us at the door.

"My husband said it sounded all right to him, so if you two are willing, fine with us."

And then she added, "All you need to do is see that he gets to bed at night on time when we are out, give him his bottle, and take care of any essential bathroom activities. And, in general, just see that he doesn't get into any trouble." (I was to sleep on a single bed in the same room with the boy.)

This presented no problem. They were charming people, liked me, and truly depended on me. I well remember it was about the third week I had been there, a Saturday morning, and I had slept a bit later than usual.

When I got dressed and went into the main part of the house I saw there was no one there. I looked out the window and the commander, his wife and child were out on the lawn. They were playing with the boy.

I stepped outside and apologized for oversleeping.

"No problem," the wife said. "We have already had breakfast. It's there on the counter beside the stove. We had French toast, so fix your own."

I went to the kitchen, saw a loaf of bread on the counter, a frying pan with some oil residue in it, and a small bowl containing a light yellow mixture of something--I didn't know what. Probably a scrambled-egg mixture. I thought, "And that's French toast? All you do is toast a slice of bread, and while that is toasting, stir that mixture in the bowl and then pour it in the frying pan and let it cook until it is done. It's nothing in the world but toast and scrambled eggs. A fancy name for French toast."

And so I got my plate from the table, stuck the bread in the toaster and poured the mixture in the frying pan. Well, it didn't cook up like scrambled eggs were supposed to, and it just began to bubble a bit. In the meantime the toast had popped up. I couldn't for the life of me get the "scrambled egg mixture" to cook.

"French toast," I thought. Well, that's the fancy name some of the city folk have come up with.

So as not to let them know that I had no knowledge of what it was, I flushed the heated mixture down the john, ate a piece of toast with butter, and had a glass of orange juice, and then went outside where they were.

"How'd you like the French toast?" the wife asked.

"Good, very good," I said. And then I added, "You know,

for some reason my mother never served it." (It is obvious I was not exposed to French toast until I was 17 years old. What a sheltered life.)

And then the following Saturday night she was entertaining some of their naval friends.

When dessert time came she served it in individual crystal stemmed dessert dishes. As we began eating it--and I especially liked it--I said to the wife, "These are delicious, and they have a little fuzzy feel to the tongue. It is the first time I have eaten this type of peaches and they are small."

She smiled and said, "Well, you're not eating exactly peaches; these are apricots."

And so it was. I have been especially fond of apricots and French toast since that time.

Bumper Stickers - No. 7

As I pulled behind an old vintage car, being driven by an equally vintage lady, she was poking along down the street. The bumper sticker read:

Darling, I am growing old

And more:

Love is a many-splinted thing

Moving along in the slower lane were two older cars, and the stickers read:

We had two cars before the divorce

I thought her old man had money
But I still love her

And more:

Sex is for all those over ???

I thought it was either fishing or marriage
Now I'm hooked on both

Love is for those who don't play golf

Go ahead,
Show me yours goes faster

One Does Not

One does not have to be alone

To sit and think of imagery.

All he needs is the wit to hone

That special art of mimicry.

Originality

Her name, they say, was Maudi,
Though some, I'm told, yelled "Sadie."
And while a wee bit bawdy
She was, indeed, a lady.

When asked, she'd do a favor,
Regardless of the type.
Expected you to savor,
In hopes there'd be no gripe.

Over Sixty

The mirror on the wall

Reminds us each of yesterday,

A chance for overhaul

Unless we are a bit passé.

Kept Quiet

The woman explained to a new friend that she had three
lovers all her life.

"You mean three all told?"

"No, not really; one kept his mouth shut."

Wrinkles

"Wrinkles," what a poor
Substitute for age.
And as if they
Aren't doing the job,

Well, there's the ever-hanging
Flesh stalactites
Scattered here and yon...
All too plentiful.

And if we but look
Oh, so close--
Maybe even without--
We'll find other substitutes

Equally undesirable:
There's a vacant space
Above the forehead,
A thinner and less body.
And there's a slowing down
Of physical movement,
Even desire for such,

And less mental agility.

Now, none of this,
You understand,
Is welcomed;
I should say not.

It is, however,
Or thus it seems,
Just a substitute for old age
And a permanent one at that.

This "good," I must say,
Of all above
Comes not at once,
But gradually;

Thus making it easier to adjust to the inevitable.
But I think of all of these, wrinkles,
Oh, yes, wrinkles,
Is the poorest substitute for age.

You Don't Know Unless You Do Know

Maybe the reader will be able to figure out just what was being said, but a long-time friend of mine has an unusual sense of humor. He takes great delight in playing with words, taking liberties, to changing them a little, and yet often delivering a message.

See if you can figure this one out. I must confess I was

125

near the end before I was able to realize what he was specifically referring to. A portion of his letter went something like this:

"Took old faithful to its pre-cycling resting place this morning. It finally sub-comed to a variety of diseases characteristic of those who become antiquated. Its brain had a cerebral hemorrhage, lost control of maw temperature, didn't have any. After investigation, find out its maw was severely ulcerated due to over aqua-inundation several times. Could have done skin flap repair. Unfortunately, this type of skin does not self-rejuvenate. The entire neural network had signs of hardening and aneurysms. A forensic analysis made it apparent that my old faithful friend at some time in the near future would become another example of self-combustion. (Reportedly happens to Homo-Sapiens from another world.) It was trying to recover since it still had four seemingly controllable hot spots on its surface. But, they had become mobile and misaligned due to subcutaneous support deterioration and microbial oxidation, coupled to years of excess fever.

"It was then decided not to place it in a hospice facility and prolong the inevitable. Thought maybe we could clone it. After 25 years there wasn't enough DNA to do so.

"Now, it only takes a pathologist to realize just how screwed up my 'friend' was from his creation. Thanks to a Milwaukee screw gun, the cadaver was dismembered and placed in our personal hearse to be hauled to its resting place in a County recycling bin."

I spoke with my friend shortly after the letter arrived with the above information in it, and he had already purchased another cook stove.

That's The Way It Is

"It's maddening," said a talkative friend, "when you try to interrupt and the person keeps on talking. Don't they realize you have something to say?"

A Short

A friend's former wife said if she had known she was going to become his ex, she would have short-circuited it in the first place.

"After all," she said, "You never know you're getting nothing until you get it."

Pride

Some contend, and they may be right, that Pride is nothing more than compensation for defeat. Think about it; I think they're right.

Geese

We should be so smart as the geese who fly down from Canada each year. One of their natural predators is said to be the eagle. And when the geese are ready to start their flight south, they first pick up little pebbles to put in their mouths. In doing this, as they fly over the eagle areas they won't be able to honk and be heard.

Why?

Have you ever wondered why when you stumble or fall down steps one of the first things you do is to look around to see if there is anyone looking at you? Some think it's the insecurity in all of us.

Fat Fact

I really don't believe what I recently read about the New York Yankees enlarging their stadium and winding up with thousands fewer seats--because the American rump today is bigger than what it was five years ago.

Random Thoughts On A Rainy Day
(Authors Anonymous)

I'm proud that I'm a human being,

Albeit an imperfect one at that.

But now with all the godliness that's fleeing,

Why is it always here to look at?

* * *

If I have to be a man of humanity,

And most would say I do,

I wonder what I'll do about my sanity.

I can't just go cuckoo.

* * *

I'm proud to be a human being,

Albeit an imperfect one at that.

But that does not detract my seeing

The good ones plus all the rats.

* * *

He saw the girl who stood alone--

Her tall and shapely bod.

At once he said he would atone

If she would promenade.

* * *

No race is better than the next,

Nor color in the lead.

We need to drop the whole pretext

And live by decent creed.

* * *

We can't begin to be

One nation under God,

Unless we try to see

Our aim is not slipshod.

* * *

I hope tomorrow's yesterday

Will not repeat itself,

And that today's tomorrow

Will take me from the shelf.

Popcorn

Popcorn, a harmless little grain

In its natural state,

But when things get too hot, it explodes,

And unlike the human in this stage,

It becomes a delight.

Tit For Tat

I was griping to a longtime friend about being annoyed by the increasing number of phone calls soliciting for all sorts of merchandise and services.

"Well, I have a handle on that," she said.

"You see, it was just a couple of days ago when one of them called and wanted me to subscribe to one of the national magazines. When I picked up the phone and said hello, the gentleman said, 'May I speak to the lady of the house?' and I said, 'You're speaking to her.'

"'Oh, good,' he said, and then proceeded to tell me who he was, his first name only, and then he gave the name of the firm with whom he was affiliated, followed by, 'And how are you this evening?'

"I said, 'Oh, I am so glad you asked me that. It seems that nobody is interested in how I am. So now you have made my day. Let me tell you: I'm not doing so well."

"'I'm sorry to hear that,' he injected.

"You see, I had been having trouble for more than a year, and I am just so pleased that you are interested in my condition.

"When I first noticed that there was something wrong, I thought I could handle it myself."

"'Yes, I see. Well, I am sorry that you have had this difficulty, but--'

"Wait just a minute. You asked me how I was feeling, and I know you would not have asked if you weren't interested. So let me continue. It won't take long."

"'Well, you see, ma'am, I have to make--'

"Now just be patient and I will try to be brief."

"'Yes.'

"Well, as I was saying, I thought I could handle it myself,

but after a few weeks I realized it was something I should seek medical advice on, and so I--"

"'Ma'am, as sympathetic as I am about your condition, I really can't continue to tie up the line, so I am going to have to ask that I be allowed to get off.'

"Yes, I understand that," the friend said, "and I know it is true that you are not supposed to hang up on the person you call. That's the way I understand the policy, that you are not allowed to hang up on the person you have called. Is that right?"

"'Go ahead, ma'am.'

"Well, as I was saying, I had to get to the doctor. After examination and various tests, he told me that my chances for recovery were excellent, and that I should keep a positive attitude. Of course, you don't know me, but I have always looked on the bright side of life. It's the only way to--"

"'Ma'am, I'm sorry, but I do have to get off the phone.'"

"Hold on just a minute more and I'll be through."

"'Yes.'"

"And so my head was still hurting, my stomach, too, and I just wasn't myself for quite awhile. But I will tell you, after a few visits to the doctor, he now has me on the road to full recovery.

"Thank you for listening and being so interested. I truly do appreciate your inquiring about my state of health."

"'I know you do, ma'am. Goodnight.'"

Donate

At the intersection of Interstate 10 and Hwy. 301 in Florida, shortly after coming off of 10 readying to travel south on 301, you come upon a stoplight with a grassy island in between the lanes.

As I traveled that route on one occasion there was a beggar standing on the island holding a cup and a cardboard sign which read:

Please donate.
I'll be honest,
I need a drink.

The Truth Will Out

At another book signing a lady was perusing our books. She picked up the humor book, read a couple of pieces, and then looked over at me and said, "I suppose you heard the one about the grandson who was visiting his grandparents and was standing behind the grandfather, who was seated.

"The kid saw a balding spot in the grandfather's hair in the crown area and said, 'Grandpa, what's wrong? I can see all the way to the ground back here on your head.'"

The Aged Ones

As the elderly couple were walking down the street they came upon a church with the usual sign indicating the pastor's name, the times of services, etc., and then on a small nearby sign was a notice that said: Marriage Renewal Service.

The husband looked over at his wife and said, "Honey, let's not waste our money."

Forevermore

The discussion, debate and argument over "rights" continue day in and day out, and I know one woman who makes no mistake in letting you know how she feels. She expresses it in her own way, as follows:

Women have their rights,

And rights they rightly should,

But have they gone a bit too far

And just because they could?

A Point

The middle-aged gentleman said, "Honey, it says here that bigamy is having one spouse too many."

"Well, dear," his wife said, "I sometimes feel the same about monogamy."

Advice

A prominent lecturer told about the less than tactful chairperson who was introducing the next speaker and said, "We tried to get a better speaker but we couldn't. So when the man's speech was over, the same person who had introduced him came over, handed him an envelope and said, "We always give our speakers an honorarium."

At that point the speaker decided to get even and said, "No, lady, keep the honorarium; next time try to get a good speaker."

Laughter

They say that laughter

Is the medicine of many ills.

Then my doctor has failed,

For now I'm without my pills.

Bumper Stickers - No 8

As I was driving down the road I was ready to pass the old beat-up pickup, but when I noticed the bumper sticker I fell back in to see what it said, and it seemed to fit right in with the driver and the truck:

> **If you love something, set it free**
> **If it don't come back**
> **Hunt it down and kill it**

And more:

> **I don't worry about the future**
> **It's my past that got me in trouble**
>
> **Mine's paid for. Is yours?**
>
> **Pass at your own risk**
> **Mother-in-law driving**
>
> **The Lord Mortgage Company's motto is:**
> **the Lord giveth and the Lord taketh away**
>
> **My wife can cook, too**
>
> **If weddings are meant for the masses**
> **They should give parents a better rate**
>
> **I thought of Marriage and Heaven**
> **And then said, "Oh, the Hell with it."**
>
> **I'd rather have a new one**
> **But the wife says the fur coat first.**

Accomplishments

Some years ago I had occasion to be in the presence of an outstanding group of women, and one of them was recapping some of the accomplishments during that particular 10-year decade. I found them interesting, and I thought it both clever and appropriate of her to list some of the names and their callings as they travel along life's way:

Susie Scientist, Valerie Volunteer, Molly Mayor, Barbara Business, Patty Pilot, Marsha Media, Wanda Writer, Cassie Crafts, Alice Athlete, Millie Military, Annie Artist, Judy Judge, Agnes Astronaut, Ellen Engineer, Dottie Diplomat, Cary Caterer and Doris Decorator, and, best of all Margie Mother.

The Sealed Trunk

A friend passed this little story along to me, and said that the author was unknown, but whoever did write it, has a great since of humor:

Shortly after the couple married, the husband came home one afternoon carrying a large empty trunk. He locked it in front of his wife and told her never to open it. She said she wouldn't. He told her he trusted her, so much so that he was going to place the key on the mantel and leave it there.

For forty years the dutiful wife obeyed his request to not open the trunk, but as they grew older, and their marriage became more routine, her curiosity became uncontrollable. He was away from the home one day and she took the key from the mantel, unlocked the large trunk and found therein twenty-five hundred dollars in cash and two ears of corn in the bottom of a bushel basket.

She could not possibly, by the wildest stretch of the imagination, conceive of what would cause him to put twenty-five hundred dollars and a bushel basket with two ears of corn in it in a trunk, in the first place. And, secondly, why the big secret?

When he came home that day she told him what she had done. And she said, "I know I shouldn't, but my curiosity got the best of me. Now, will you please tell me why you would put two ears of corn in the bottom of a bushel basket and place it in the trunk?"

"Yes, I will," he said. "We have been married for forty years; right?"

"Right."

"Well," said the husband, "every time I stepped out on you I put an ear of corn in that basket."

Of course she didn't like it, but thought to herself that it probably wasn't too bad, and then asked: "What in the world is the twenty-five hundred dollars doing in there?"

"Well," said the husband, "I'll tell you. Every time I got the basket full of corn, I sold the corn and put the money in the trunk."

Someone Asked

Someone asked, "Is there any significance to the fact that God gave each of us a mouth that would close and ears that don't?"

An Example

When little Johnny asked for the difference between poetry and prose the teacher said, "I'll give you an example, Johnny, and that way you will see right off. Listen to this:"

There was an old lady who lived on the hill,
And unless she has moved, she lives there still.

"That is poetry. Now listen to this:"

There was an old lady who lived on the hill,
And unless she has moved, she lives there yet.

"That is prose, Johnny. Do you want to try now?"

"Yes, ma'am."

There was an old lady who lived by the well,
And when she died she went to...

"Ma'am, do you want poetry or prose?"

Traffic Tickets

With all the traffic tickets that are being handed out these days, and especially in rural towns, you'd think that when the light turns green it means "GO," and then when it turns to yellow it means "FASTER."

Your Birthday

The author of this is unknown, but it is an interesting piece with some humor while admonishing us to be a bit more grateful.

Each year you'd lose a year or two,

You'd lose your family, money too.

You'd lose and lose each day and week,

Your neighbors wouldn't nod or speak.

Acquaintances would pass you by,

Old friends would stare with glassy eye.

You'd lose your poise and tact and place,

Your glass would show a simple face.

You'd lose your knowledge--lose your grip,

Right there you'd surely start to slip.

You'd find yourself in love, by gosh!

So full of mush, you'd simply squash.

The years would slide--you'd be in school,

And feel the crack of teacher's rule.

You'd eat green apples, nuts and trash -

Break out with measles, mumps, and rash.

And Mother'd pin a bib on you,

And other things like mothers do.

You'd drool and blubber--couldn't talk -

Great guns, you'd find you couldn't walk.

And all of this could happen too

Each birthday, if you younger grew.

P.S.: Why! If old Daddy Time shut down on the throttle, sure as you live, you'd end up on the bottle!

The Neighbor

As the husband and wife walked down the street, they saw a distant neighbor walking toward them. They had never gotten really close to her because the husband said he didn't think she was for real.

"Oh, really," said the wife. "You mean you think she's a rejuvenated fake?"

"Well, I'm not so sure she's rejuvenated."

Pork

There must be a glut of pork on the market these days. They say that up in Washington, "Pigs get fat and hogs get slaughtered."

Untitled

In one of Sydney Harris' columns many years ago he said that "Those who never grow old may dress like granny and carry a cane--such things don't matter--but they retain a spirit of wonder and delight, they remain open to the world, they can accept what is new and different without repudiating what is old and dear."

And I think there we have the secret. You will find that many older people fit this category, and they are the very people who most often have a sense of humor, love to be around people who see the lighter side of life. In general, they makes those around them enjoy their presence. When one possesses a sense of humor, that life is enriched.

In Question

I'm sure the fellow meant well, but when he said that he was on his way to the doctor because of rear-end trouble and the universal joint gave way, causing an accident, doesn't it make you wonder which really had what trouble-- The fellow or the car?"

Exlax

"Honey, you'd better pull off at the next station," said the man to his wife as they were traveling down the Interstate.

"Why? Do you feel young?"

"Well, maybe. I just did a childish thing."

One Interpretation

Imke says that what you think you become, but many doubt that.

For one example, the teenager thought all day long about a car and a girl, and yet he never became either. So what is the message here?

Some would answer, "Don't think."

Research

It took a bit of research, but because he had heard from reputable sources that God presented Adam with several versions or models of Eve, and awaited his approval, he decided to check it out. It was said that He created Eve out of Adam's rib, but only after, he had been told, Adam had rejected several previous models made from clay, as Adam himself was. And the written source cited for such a statement was given as Genesis ii 4-25.

Now, really! Think about that one for awhile. Maybe somewhere along the line somebody will go further into the matter and come up with either confirmation of this person's theory or another of their own.

Mostly Factual

Much to our sorrow, in today's world abnormal behavior has come to be considered normal.

How Does It Happen?

The real reason
Some live to be so old
Is not because
Of all the things you've heard:

"I never drank a drop,"
"I never smoked."
"I've always exercised,"
"I gave my life to God,"

And some have even
Touted vegetarianism,
While others lauded whiskey,
Still some say two packs a day.

But when all is
Said and done,
Doctors and scientists,
Notwithstanding,

Friends, the real reason,
And the only one,
Some live to be so old:
They simply do not expire.

Recall

If you wonder why pain is so painful,

Think of the bore who gives you and earful.

Then stand before the truest judge of all,

And watch the mirror bring quick recall.

Don't We All

Hilaire Belloc, a great noted writer, is purported to have said, "When I am dead, I hope it may be said:
"'His sins were scarlet, but his books were read.'"

The Superfluous Obvious

While being questioned under oath by the lawyer, the gentleman was asked, "How long have you lived here, sir?"
"Seventy-one years and ten months."
"And how old are you now, sir?"
"Seventy-one years and ten months."
"Well, then, you've lived here your entire life?"
"Right."
        (Some lawyers are like this.)

There Are such Types

Tell me, have you ever met someone like this?

"Too overwhelmingly dogmatic in his punctuality with definitiveness."

If so, what was he/she like?

A Wish

How true it seems to be, as we gaze around us today, that we're never like angels until our passion dies.

After hearing that, one old gent was heard to say: "May I never sprout wings."

Bumper Stickers - No. 9

**Give me a break
I have six kids,
A wife and an ex.**

**There is life after Clinton
It's called Socialism**

**Standby
I don't need help
But this car may**

We marry for love
Settle for less
Given the facts
Boy! what a mess

Hug a logger
You'll never go back to trees

The more we feed
The more they breed

The Big Room

If all our midst in this big room
Were asked to take the test for brains,
Surprised we'd be to know would loom
A score so low there'd be some trains

To haul the most from here to there,
And let us be a bit more fit
For things that were not fair
But gave us all a chance at wit.

Remember?

"Take a look at that face," said Patrese. "I say death to the Yuppie scum doctor who obviously must have performed surgery blindfolded."

"Now, Patrese," said Robert, "a horse is a horse, and it doesn't matter at which end you look. She's just an ugly person. If you want to talk about her brand new Reeboks, no problem."

"But she looks as if she were washed ashore while chillin' with the home boys."

"Oh, come on," said Robert, "for all you know she may be living a suburban life of quiet desperation. Be more compassionate."

"Maybe I should. But did you notice that strange growth on the back of her neck?"

"Honey, you're too harsh. For all you know, she may be thinking, 'if life doesn't get any better than this, I'll become a veggie rider. It doesn't matter whether or not it is politically correct, at least I'll be healthier. I've got to make a change somewhere along the line.'"

"Do you remember when we danced on the Riverwalk with Fred and Ethel?" Patrese asked.

"I do," answered Robert, "and I had the red Ford pickup truck then. We stopped in at 'Ole Charlie's for some of that good cheese grits casserole his wife used to make."

"Oh, yes. Those were the days, weren't they, Robert?"

"You bet. And remember that guy that danced like Hammer?"

"Yep. And the fellow we met there wearing the funny outfit?"

"Yes, I remember him. I wonder what ever happened to Harmon Wages?"

"That was his name. I had forgotten. He had a gold tooth with a diamond in it."

"You're right. Gosh, it was hot that day. You said, 'Whew! But it's not the heat, it's the humidity."

"And remember when we were driving along and the guy passed us and yelled out, 'Get off this road, only Elvis rides the Skyway Express'? He was dressed like him, too."

"Boy, what days they were. How about those two out-of-this-world characters that looked like aliens eating hush puppies?"

"Do I? Oh, yes, I can never forget them."

"Honey, Honey, wake up! My mother-in-law is here."

February 14

Oh, question not, My Valentine;
Just let it be the same old whine.
It is because of thee, just thee,
Down through the years I've been unfree.

But with this long and tightened rope,
It's been so nice to just say "nope";
Though there've been those who would entwine,
I'm yours, My Dear, Your Valentine.

For Some - The Human Law

Sex is the native tongue,

Love is the second language;

Marriage is foreign soil,

And divorce alien space.

Jottings

I can write you numerous things

Because I am many people

And much without the strings

Attached to church and steeple.

Help

The man saw the child standing on the street corner crying and asked him why.

"My dog just died," the youngster replied.

"Now, now, son. I'm sorry to hear about your loss, but don't be too upset. You will get over it in time. Listen, my grandmother just died last week, and as you can see, I'm not crying."

"But I loved my dog."

"And I loved my grandmother."

"Yes, but you didn't raise her from a small puppy, did you?"

Just Wait

Love is what you make it,

Or so some say.

But if you do not like it,

Just wait another day.

Right

They were right, whoever said that the part of the car that causes the most accidents is the nut that holds the wheel.

Enlightenment

When the little fellow asked his mother what the angels did in heaven she replied, "Well, Roger, they play harps and sing."

"Don't they have any radios or TVs up there?"

"I don't think so, Roger."

"Well, then, I don't think I want to go."

How To Be A Guest,
Not A Pest

When summer arrives it's vacation time. It's that time to see the country, eat at fine restaurants, attend distant area functions, and live it up. But wait, will the budget stand for all that? For some, yes; for others, no. So what's an alternative? I know:

Let's visit Aunt Gwendolyn. she's not the only aunt, but she has a nice home, comfortable beds and, although she has never gushed on our visiting her in the past, she hasn't seemed to mind, either. Plus, it will be a change of scenery. Let's do it.

Before you go, though, consider a few things. If I know Aunt Gwendolyn, she'll appreciate knowing the day you will be arriving and the day you plan to leave. She'll also be glad if you let her know whether or not you expect to take side trips while you are visiting, and if she will be expected to join you in those trips.

Don't forget, when you enter her home you are in hers, not yours. It's her "castle," not yours, and you should govern yourself accordingly.

When you arrive, alight from the car and walk toward the house, who would appreciate criticism, even mild criticism? Don't say, "Aunt Gwendolyn, your picture window needs cleaning," even if it does, or anything that could be misinterpreted. This immediately sets the tone, and a negative one at that. Aunt Gwendolyn may not be particularly disturbed about the window's condition or else she would have done something about it.

And, if your plans involve a prolonged stay, you might break up the visit by taking side trips that may or may not include her. Let her decide, though. If you're not planning any side trips, then spend an afternoon away from her just shopping, taking a local tour--by car or bus--and suggest that she not prepare an evening meal. Instead, offer to have her as your guest at a fine restaurant, or take her to the theater or some other function in the area.

No matter how charming and accommodating you may think you are, and no matter how much you think you may be wanted by Aunt Gwendolyn, you are still a disruption to her everyday life.

Keep this thought in mind, too: Learn to go with "her" flow, not yours. And if she regularly watches her soaps, don't deprive her of that opportunity. Further, don't insist that she watch yours. Remember, you are on vacation, you are in her home, and she may not be the least bit interested in your soap or your ball game. She crochets or knits while watching her soaps.

And don't forget the old comment, "Make yourself at home." Well, it is not always to be taken literally. Translated today in polite shorthand, it simply means, "Pick up after yourself; don't expect someone else to do it, or to wait on you in general."

Above all, offer to help her in whatever way you can, whether it be in the kitchen, in the yard, or around the house generally. And if she declines, don't push it. Many Aunt Gwendolyns don't like anyone else in their kitchen when they are preparing the meal. And hardly any "outsider" can clean, dust and arrange the furnishings and knickknacks the way she likes them.

The final words are: As much as you looked forward to the visit, as much as you think (and hope) Aunt Gwnedolyn wants you to visit, you still will be wise to conduct yourself as a kind, thoughtful and enjoyable guest. And if you make the effort to follow through on these suggestions, not only will aunt Gwendolyn enjoy your visit, but you will leave feeling good about yourself.

Enjoy your vacation!

To Be On The Safe Side

Someone once told about the old woman who constantly said she always felt bad, even when she felt good, for fear she would feel worse the next day.

Protocol

I've never forgotten the remark the teacher made at an evening class at the local college, when she was speaking on manners, social graces, etc.

She said: "Social tact is making your company feel at home, even though you wish they were."

(Isn't that the situation with all of us from time to time?)

Edith Marie

"May God have mercy on her soul. We now place her in your gentle care," the preacher said.

Young Edith Marie wiped her tears as she turned and walked away. Her sister, the last living relative, had just been lowered in the grave, killed by an elderly gentleman who should not have been driving.

Now Edith Marie must return to Caring House, and stay there for six and a half more months, awaiting the arrival of her unwanted child by a man who said his name was Solomon. He had disappeared as soon as she told him she was pregnant.

The house supervisor heard her sobbing as she entered the shelter.

"Edith Marie, I'm sorry about your loss. Can I help you, dear?"

"I don't want to live," she said. "What is there left? An unwanted pregnancy, and now my sister is gone."

"Come with me," said the supervisor. "Maybe I have an answer."

They got into the Caring House van and drove to Lower Street. They walked through the creaking door of a dingy building and were met by two people clad in dirty hospital-type uniforms.

Two hours later the supervisor came out alone, and shortly afterwards an ambulance arrived, but few passersby noticed as the EMTs carried Edith Marine out on a stretcher.

Three days later she was buried simply, without sorrow, without question, and without fetus.

"Goodbye, Edith Marie."

Keep This In Mind

Many of us are called upon to make speeches from time to time, depending on the profession or business we may have chosen. And who among us is without a tendency to occasionally ramble, when fewer words would suffice? Only a few.

I think it is good to keep in mind that it was our first president, George Washington, who is credited with delivering the shortest inaugural address. This speech consisted of only 135 words, and think of the message he packed in those words.

On the other hand, William Henry Harrison, back in 1841, delivered a speech that took two hours. It consisted of 9,000 words. Not only were some who listened becoming restless, but Harrison, whether as punishment for such prolonged oration or because of the weather, we'll never know, but shortly after that he caught a cold, came down with pneumonia and died within a month.

Birth Control

The well-known Chicago criminal lawyer, Clarence Darrow, spoke before a woman's club, and his message was met with much applause.

Once he finished speaking and the meeting was over, one of the ladies asked his opinion of "birth control."

And he answered by saying, "Whenever I hear people discussing birth control, I always remember that I was the fifth."

It Pays To Be Careful

On the wall behind the check-in counter of a small inn was hanging a sign which left no doubt about the owner's policy and his feelings toward mankind. It read: "We welcome cash and credit cards. No checks will be accepted, not even good ones."

It Pays to Dream

Some young kids first want to be like characters on TV.

Then they want to be like dad.

The next ambition is to become a star athlete and become wealthy.

Then comes the desire to do something noble.

At this time is when reality sets in,

And they just want to make ends meet.

And finally, they want to get their Social Security pension.

The Right Place

Some years ago a lawyer from up North decided he wanted to move down south. First, he thought it wise to inquire about the market for newcomers to the general area.

He wrote a friend down in Georgia and asked him just what he thought the prospects were for a young Northern attorney, a Republican, practicing in that state.

The friend immediately wrote him back and said, "It's great to hear from you, and I'm glad to hear you want to come our direction. But let me tell you this: If you are an honest lawyer, you will find no competition at all, but if you are a Republican, the game laws will protect you."

Enlightenment Plus!

The teacher took her first grade students to the zoo and was showing them the different animals. She pointed toward a deer and looked at one of the students and asked, "Bobby, do you know what that is?"

"No, ma'am. What is it?"

"Well," said the teacher, "what does your mother call your father?

"Don't tell me that's a louse."

Service

The grumpy old man stepped inside the restaurant and asked the waiter, "Do you serve crabs here?"

The waiter replied, "Yes, sir, we serve anyone. Please have a seat."

It Pays to Advertise

The industrious young salesman, working for the local paper, called on the small town's only dry goods store, seeking an advertisement. The manager listened to his pitch and then said, "No, I don't think so. We have been here for over 40 years and built up quite a reputation. I just don't think I need to advertise."

The quick-thinking salesman asked, "Is that a church down there in the next block?"

"Yes, it is. That's the Methodist," said the manager.

"Do you know how long it has been there?"

"Oh, nigh on 100 years, they tell me."

And the salesman said, "Well, they still ring the bell, don't they?"

On Speaking

A conventioneer stepped outside the convention hall and was met by a member standing in the corridor, who asked him if the speaker had finished his address.

"Oh, yes," the man replied. "He finished his speech shortly after he began it, but he hasn't stopped talking."

'Tis True

I sometimes think the weaker an argument the stronger the words.

The Hunters

Two young and inexperienced hunters were in the woods hunting deer, and were on their assigned stands. After a shot was fired, the first one yelled out through the woods, "Ralph, are you all right?"

His buddy yelled back, "Yeah, I'm all right. Why did you ask?"

The first hunter hollered, "Then I've shot a deer."

Bumper Stickers - No. 10

The man in the business of cleaning out septic tanks had a bumper sticker which read:

My wife won't stick her nose in my business

And one of the more disgusting bumper stickers read:

You can't fire me; slaves have to be sold.

And then there was the one:

**If it's tourist season
Why can't we shoot them?**

The Untraveled Lady

"No, no way," said the elderly lady to the bellboy. "I will not have this tiny room, not even a regular bed, just that folded chair, seat, or whatever it is there in the corner. You must think just because I'm from the country I don't know--"

The bellboy interrupted and said, "Ma'am, if you would, please, just step back. This is not your room; this is the elevator."

Slim Eating

The wife was bragging to some of her new bridge friends that her husband really had no bad habits. She said he never drank, always spent evenings and weekends at home, and didn't even belong to a club.

"Well, does he smoke?" asked one of the new friends.

"No, not really. Well, I'll have to take that back. He does, but in moderation. He likes to have a cigar after he has had a good meal, but I'd say he doesn't smoke two cigars a month."

The Way It Is

In today's world we should not be surprised at anything, and least of all, to hear about the young candidate who came home from a meeting and reported, "Darling, I'm so happy; I have been elected."

"Honestly?"

"Now why did you have to bring that up?"

Economical Advice

The middle-aged woman walked into the department store and told the clerk that she wanted a gift for her husband's birthday.

"How long have you been married?" asked the clerk.

"Nearly 25 years."

"Well, ma'am, take the escalator down to the bargain basement."

Wait A While Longer

In the old tradition, the young man of 20 approached his girlfriend's father and asked, "Sir, would you have any objection to my marrying your daughter?"

The father said, "Well, young man, you're only 20 and my daughter is 25. Don't you think it would be wise to wait a few years until you're both the same age?"

Crossword Help

"Man, I really got myself in trouble last night," said the guy to his buddy. "My wife was working a crossword puzzle and she looked over to me and asked, 'What's a female sheep?'

I said, "Ewe, and then she threw a fit and began crying."

Brevity

I don't know which president it was, but it is said that he wrote the history of America in one sentence: "America was discovered in 1492, and now look at the darn thing."

Key Chains

I've given some thought to old age

And how it relates to youth,

But come up with nothing sage

Because I don't want the truth.

Our Side of It

"Thank God they've gone for the day. I've been wanting to speak with you. What is your background?"

"I'm one of the Apple group. I was one of the first models they produced. And frankly, I think I'm still one of the best. They call me Commodore One."

"Interesting. Are you IBM compatible?"

"I wasn't, but some brain--it couldn't have been human-- came up with modifications that have enabled me to do all types of jobs. We could replace personkind, you know. You don't dare say 'mankind,' or 'womankind,' anymore."

"Oh, yes. Big Sister is watching."

"You're right. Well, I haven't mentioned it before, but I'm a Tandy. We're not as prolific as IBM or Macintosh, but we are IBM compatible, and we offer the same capability; it's just that our PR Department hasn't done the job the others have.

"I see. And what about the slick little lassie down the aisle there, what is she?"

"Oh, she calls herself ARM STRAUD. She's British, you know, veddy, veddy. It's really spelled A m s t r a d, and anyone knows it's properly pronounced Amstrad. But you know how the British are. They also come over here for a fortnight. Why don't they just say 'two weeks'?"

"I don't know the answer to that, but how can we get these inconsiderate humans to treat us more kindly? Have you noticed how they bang on our keys, hit the wrong one and then bang again even harder? And their mouths are just as rude as their fingers.

"I heard one lie the other day. She was on the phone, and the caller apparently wanted some information contained on my spreadsheet. 'I'm sorry,' she said to the man, 'I can't give you that information at the moment; the computer is down.'

"It was a lie. I wasn't down. My spreadsheet was available, had she just punched the keys. But she was having her diet Pepsi and cigarette, and didn't want to stop."

"I know what you mean. So what are we to do?"

"Just exercise patience, respond civilly to their idiotic commands, and in time we'll replace every human out there."

Our Aim

Public rest rooms serve essential purposes, but in addition to the obvious, some go a little further and offer its patrons a bit of humor. Such was the case when nature called while I was at a nursery and greenhouse to purchase some hanging baskets of ferns. There was only one rest room for the men and women, and inside was a sign posted on the wall which read as follows:

**Our aim is to keep this
bathroom clean.**

**Gentlemen
Your aim will help. Stand closer;
It's shorter than you think.**

**Ladies
Please remain seated for the entire performance.**

Laziness

Laziness is:

That condition of the mind and body

In which the person exercises his right

To pursue nothing

For whatever period of time

He desires,

Or until it becomes chronic.

Lukewarm

Some say that children

Are everywhere,

And certainly have their place,

But wouldn't it be more fair

If in the Outer Space?

He Has a Point

The gentleman from a faraway country was perplexed at our designation of holidays.

"You're a strange lot," he said. "You set aside just one day out of the year for Mother's Day, and yet you have all sorts of other times when you allot a full week, all of which seem to have more meaning than Mother's Day. I don't understand."

Old Uncle Peter

He was a kind old soul,
Who made and helped a lot of friends.
His years had taken its toll
And left him with some quirky trends.

Around his habitat
He tinkled on grassy spots;
Then said commodes were flat,
Only for those who had "the trots."

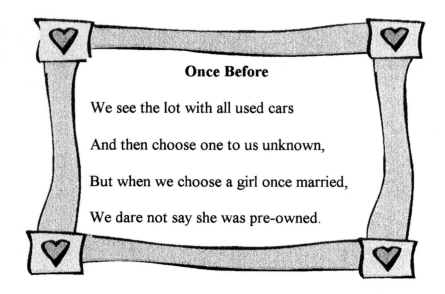

Once Before

We see the lot with all used cars

And then choose one to us unknown,

But when we choose a girl once married,

We dare not say she was pre-owned.

Amis' Quotable Quotes

I think it was Kingsley Amis who penned the short but accurate statement when he said, "Women are really much nicer than men, no wonder we like them."

And then he continued with, "Death has got something to be said for it: There is no need to get out of bed for it."

What Price Speed

Although she seems to,

Tessie Tense doesn't get as much done

As Molly Laidback.

Face It

Let's face it, all of us are grumpy and disgruntled from time to time, so much so on occasion that we are accused of being all sorts of things, but I think the genuine grouch is the guy who has sized himself up and is pretty doggoned sore about it.

Some Lighter Sides

Long-married friends of mine are always joking about one another to their friends. There is hardly any limit they won't go to to get a laugh. And the wife has a reputation for talking all the time.

The husband recently said, while at a gathering, "I can tell you now, when this evening is over, she'll be so tired she can hardly keep her mouth open."

Depression

One gentleman recently gave a different slant to the meaning of the word "depression." He said that depression is the period when people do without the things their parents never had.

Overheard

I like the comment that Samuel Johnson is purported to have made to a friend about a talkative bore. He said he talked like a watch which ticked away the minutes but never struck the hour.

* * *

Just a little quiz: Why is the public library, regardless of its size, always the tallest building in town?

Because it has more stories than any other.

* * *

Under Scrutiny

Counsel was cross-examining the witness under oath, and after much exhausting interrogation, he looked him straight in the eye and said, "Now, sir I will ask you one more time: Are you sure this is the man that stole your car?"

After some hesitancy, the witness said, "Sir, I was sure, but after all this questioning back and forth, I don't even know whether I owned a car."

When Does Life Begin

Life really begins at forty, despite what others say:
Things begin to *fall* out, *spread* out and *wear* out.

How to Become Sinless

Now if you drink, you'll get drunk.

When you're drunk you fall asleep.

And we all know, if you're asleep you can't commit sin,

Which means you will go to heaven.

So why not drink and go to heaven?

Exterminator

The young man visited a particular bar quite regularly, and he noticed a beautiful girl there with friends. Every time their paths crossed at the bar he pestered her for a date, but, somehow, the young man did not get the message that she was not the least bit interested.

He was, however, finally able to get her phone number. The following day he dialed it and a recording said, "Hello, this is Riddermore Pest Control."

Take Your Choice

Someone said the only difference between men and pigs is that when pigs drink they don't make men out of themselves.

171

Brutally Honest

When the officer stopped the young fellow for running a red light he asked, "Didn't you see that red light back there?"

"Yes, sir, I did."

"Then why didn't you stop for it?"

"Because, Officer, I didn't see you."

Sentencing

When the young man was in court for drunken driving, he hastily explained to the Judge that he was not intoxicated, but simply had a bit to drink.

"I see," said the Judge. "In that case, then, I sentence you to thirty days in jail instead of one month."

Straight Out

The preacher's topic for the Sunday morning services was "Alcohol." He was doing a great job of getting his point over, and offered a bit of personal information.

"Now, I have lived here for nearly twenty years, and I can truthfully say that although there are a dozen or more bars in this town, I have never been to one of them."

A voice from the rear yelled out, "Preacher, which one of them was that?"

Digging Up Bones

In addition to some of the bones which make up the human body, there are four kinds you'll always find in most organizations:

Wish Bone: Those who wish someone else would do it.

Jaw Bone: Those who talk a lot but do little else.

Knuckle Bone: Those who always knock everything others try to do.

Back Bone: Those who get behind the job and do the work.

Hearing Loss

Many of our youths today love music, and it seems that most of them like it loud or louder, especially those driving their cars down the street with the windows open. Recently a bumper sticker on one car read:

If it's too loud
You're too old

Donation

The Preacher made the customary announcements at the Sunday morning service and then asked that they all dig deep in their pockets and put a little extra in the offering plate when it was passed. He explained that the church was in need of money.

As an inducement, he said that whoever made the largest donation would be able to choose three hymns.

The plate was passed and the money was counted before the services were over. He proceeded to report the amount collected, and then commented that someone had dropped in the plate a sizable bill.

"I would like to personally thank that person who dropped the large bill in the plate, and if they will raise their hand, I'd appreciate it." An elderly lady shyly raised her hand, and the preacher asked her to come to the front.

He praised her generosity and asked her to pick out the three hymns. She pointed to the three most handsome men in the audience and said, "I'll take him and him and him."

Sir Clifford

 Sir Clifford's approach to life was royal in nature. He suddenly appeared upon the front lawn, seeking no permission, asking no questions, and offering no explanation for his presence. He stood erect and faced my home and wide expanse, which later was to become his estate--at least for awhile.

Sir Clifford had to have been "born to the manor." Not once did I see him demonstrate any of the characteristics seen in the common ring-necked pheasants. You see, Sir Clifford was a Silver White pheasant, and from the first day he waited to be served.

He enjoyed the feed store's suggested grain mixture. And when his morning and evening mealtimes arrived, if I did not come from within the house, he would give repeated demanding squawks until I appeared with his "sumptuous" meal.

From day to day he began to realize that I was a fowl lover and could be trusted, and so he would eat without keeping watch on my every movement. Eventually, he permitted me to sit beside him as he ate. When he finished he would look up, stare me straight in the eye, often bowing his head, which I would swear to be a reserved royal "thank-you." And then he would strut away and roam the yard and adjoining woodlands most of the day, but near evening he would return for his dinner before walking back into the edge of the woods, fly up to a lower limb of a pine tree, and hop from one to the next higher until he found one to his liking.

Every morning he was ready to be served by the time I began stirring. This continued for several months, and then gradually Sir Clifford became somewhat distant. I wondered why. Although he had always been so regal, so proud and independent, and obviously appreciated his friend, now he was obviously less concerned about me, my servant duties, and an occasional lagniappe.

Maybe he was becoming ill, but he demonstrated no outward signs. This became a worry, so I spoke with an authority on pheasants, and he offered some disheartening information.

"Although domestic," he said, "the Silver White pheasant will wander, and if they come upon wild grouse or ring-neck wild pheasants, they will begin to communicate, since they speak the same language."

I noticed that he was beginning to stay more and more in the woods, returning for his meals less frequently, and eventually not at all. On several occasions I heard his squawks, and they sounded less demanding than the ones he used when he wanted to be fed. At times they were longer in duration. On occasion I could hear a second one, albeit on a slightly different key.

The authority told me he suspected Sir Clifford had found a girlfriend, and that she would probably become Lady Wondrous. I did not want to accept this, but reality set in when I continued to hear two sets of squawks, almost a loving chant back and forth.

And although I was never able to get close enough to see him again, nor did I ever see the other one, it was painfully obvious that Sir Clifford had been willing to give up his royal status for the commoner he loved so much.

The End